going places

Southeast England

Kent
Sussex

Titles in this Series

going places

Southeast England

Kent
Sussex

J F Straker

The Publishing Division of
The Royal Automobile Club
83-85 Pall Mall   London

First published 1981

An RAC publication

Every effort has been made to ensure that the information given in this publication is accurate and up to date, and is, to the best of our knowledge, correct at the time of going to press. However, the RAC cannot accept any responsibility for errors or omissions.

The 12 tour commentaries and accompanying maps in this book have been chosen, planned and written by the author and not by the RAC.

ISBN 0 86211 002 5

Cover picture: Nymans Gardens

Designed and produced for the RAC by
Walter Oliver Publishing Services
Illustrations by Ed Perera
Typeset by Print Things Ltd
Printed and bound by Ebenezer Baylis & Son Limited
The Trinity Press, Worcester, and London

Made and printed in Great Britain

Contents

The National Trust

There are hundreds of places of outstanding artistic and archeological interest in the 'RAC Going Places' series which are under the care of the National Trust. If you write to them at 42 Queen Anne's Gate, London SW1 you can get full information on how to join and thereby save a considerable sum in entry fees to their properties

Introduction

If Kent is the Garden of England then Sussex is its Parkland, for Sussex is more wooded than any other English county. Taken together the two counties form a region of woodland and grassland, of orchards and hop-gardens and small farms, of nature reserves and picturesque villages, of old castles and splendid country houses; a region of gentle beauty rather than of grandeur which, although often hilly, is devoid of great heights and vast expanses of desolate moorland.

Topography

Diagonally across the centre lies the Weald, once the great impenetrable Forest of Anderida – the Andredsweald, the uninhabited forest – home of the deer and the wild hog. Now it is a rich agricultural plain dotted with woodland, with the forests of Ashdown (Tour 7) and St Leonards (Tour 10) in Sussex, of Challock (Tour 2) and Blean (Tour 1) in Kent, giving only a vague idea of how it must have looked to the early invaders, Romans, Saxons, Danes and Normans, when they landed. It is at its widest in Sussex, extending southward from the Surrey border to encompass all but the South Downs and the narrow coastal strip beyond; as it stretches eastward through Kent it gradually narrows, to end on the borders of Romney Marsh (Tour 5).

In Kent there is both High Weald and Low Weald; the High Weald to the south, which continues into Sussex, is woodland and pasture country, the northern Low Weald being a region of orchards and hop-gardens, which flourish in the clay soil. Hops are grown in 'gardens', not 'fields', because in the past tithes had to be paid on the latter but not on the former. The Low Weald is lovely in all the seasons but is at its best in spring and late summer. A sea of blossom floats above the orchards in spring, although it can ebb all too quickly for the visitor. Late summer is the season for hop picking. Hops have been grown in Kent and East Sussex since their introduction into this country by Henry VIII early in the 16th century: although later he ordered their cultivation to cease, Queen Mary I later rescinded the order. Most of the small domestic oasts have disappeared; but the rows of large oasts of the big brewers around Beltinge and Paddockwood and elsewhere are familiar landmarks in the Low Weald, and the early autumn air is still strong with the smell of drying hops.

It is not only the Weald that the two counties have in common. Each has its rolling hills of chalk. In Kent the North Downs extend from the Surrey border to the coast between

Dover and Hythe. Sussex has its South Downs, stretching from the Hampshire border to end at Beachy Head. They are narrower, with fewer habitations than the North Downs. Each county has its low-lying southern coastal strip: Sussex the narrow region from the Selsey Peninsula to the eastern levels: Kent the Romney and Walland Marshes. Each county is around one million acres in area, with Kent fractionally the larger. Each has its string of seaside resorts, with Brighton the queen of them all in size and popularity. Each has its ancient castles and historic houses, although the history of the region as a whole has resulted in their being more numerous in Kent. All round the coast tidal estuaries attract a wide variety of seabirds; nature reserves and scenic areas abound, most of them maintained by the National Trust. The fact that nowhere in either county is more than 75 miles from London as the crow flies has resulted in the Southeast becoming largely a dormitory and leisure centre for commuters – although West Sussex, with its less extensive road and rail facilities, has suffered (if suffered be the word) less in this respect than has the rest of the region.

For administrative purposes Sussex is now divided into two counties by a line running roughly from East Grinstead south to between Shoreham and Hove. Kent has a more ephemeral divison: east of the Medway are the Men of Kent, with the Kentish Men to the west. The origin of this distinction is obscure; but just as Kent has tended to look down on Sussex as the more backward of the two counties (and historically this is true, for development began in the east and spread only slowly westward) so have the Men of Kent been inclined to consider themselves generally superior to Kentish Men – an attitude with less to support it.

As with most regions bordered by the sea and affected by its tides, over the years the southeast coastline of England has suffered change, with the sea encroaching in places and receding in others. The old village of Selsey in Sussex now lies under the sea, together with its Saxon cathedral. The southern marshlands were constantly being eroded. In the great storm at the end of the 13th century much of the old port of Winchelsea was washed away, forcing the townspeople to move inland, and the Rother, which had previously entered the sea at New Romney (Tour 5), was diverted to find a new outlet at Rye (Tour 5). In Roman and Saxon times Thanet was a true island, separated from the mainland of Kent by the Wantsum, a wide channel providing a short cut for ocean-going vessels plying between the English Channel and the Thames Estuary. Now the Wantsum is little more than a reedy ditch and Thanet an island

in name only.

The sea has not been the only predator. In 1965 the north-west corner of Kent was taken from the county and added to Greater London, turning Bromley and Orpington and other towns in the area into yet more suburbs of the metropolis.

History
Early Settlers
Because of its long and lively history, the southeast of England is full of reminders of the past, Kent more so than Sussex. The earliest known inhabitant is the Swanscombe Man, who lived in the marshes of the Thames Estuary in Palaeolithic times a quarter of a million years ago, hunting elephant and bison. Some of the clipped flints he used can be seen in the Swanscombe Museum, but only a few fragments of a skull remain to tell us what he was like. Traces of a later Stone Age can be seen in the impressive Coldrum Long Barrow near Trottiscliffe (Tour 6) or at Kit's Coty north of Aylesford (Tour 3); the open chamber of a long barrow on the hillside at Kit's Coty is perhaps the most famous archaeological relic in the Southeast. On Oldbury Hill, above Ightham on the Sevenoaks ridge, is an Iron Age camp constructed around 100 BC, the ramparts of which were probably used in defence against the Romans in Claudius's invasion of AD 43. Cissbury Ring (Tour 11) and Chanctonbury Ring, north of Worthing, were Iron Age forts, although because of the nature of the terrain Sussex provides less evidence than Kent of such antiquity. Other than the sites, however, little remains of the forts and settlements and barrows built by the inhabitants in pre-Roman times. Bigbury, on the hills west of Canterbury, is perhaps the best known of the hill-forts, but it is overgrown and difficult to distinguish.

The Roman Age
It is with the coming of the Romans that the history of the Southeast really commences. Historians disagree about where exactly Julius Caesar landed in 55 BC, but it is generally accepted that it was somewhere between Deal and Hythe. It was probably more of a reconnaissance than a serious attempt to conquer, and it was the invasion of Claudius nearly 100 years later that marked the real beginning of the Roman occupation. Claudius landed in Pegwell Bay, as did many subsequent invaders, and made his headquarters at Richborough, the Roman Rutupiae (Tour 1). Then an island on the southern side of the Wantsum, Richborough was easy to defend and an ideal base from which to tackle the conquest of Britain.

The Romans stayed in Britain until the middle of the 5th century, although in gradually decreasing numbers. They built

towns and settlements and made inroads into the Weald –
mainly in Kent, where the forest belt was narrower. The exca-
vations of the Roman Palace and gardens at Fishbourne near
Chichester (Tour 12) and of the magnificent Roman villas at
Lullingstone near Farningham and at Bignor in Sussex (Tour
12) give an excellent picture of their way of life in Britain. Stane
Street in Sussex, on which the A29 is roughly based, and
Watling Street, now the A2, that runs from Dover to Canterbury and on to London, are examples of how they tried to open
up the country. To keep out the Saxon pirates who began to
harass the coast during the 4th century they built forts along
what was known as the Saxon Shore, which extended south
from the Wash round to Southampton Water. In the Southeast
there were forts at Reculver, Richborough, Dover, Hythe
(Tour 5) and Pevensey (Tour 8). The commanding general,
who went under the imposing title of 'Count of the Saxon
Shore', had his headquarters at Richborough, with the 2nd
Legion stationed both here and at Reculver to command either
end of the Wantsum.

Saxons and Danes
With the withdrawal of the last Roman garrison from Britain in
442 the Southeast became the prey of the Saxons. They landed
at Ebbsfleet under Hengist and Horsa and established themselves in the Isle of Thanet; and from there they proceeded to
conquer the two counties. The next 150 years is shrouded in
mystery, but in 597 St Augustine was sent to Britain by Pope
Gregory to convert the inhabitants to Christianity. He too
landed at Ebbsfleet; he established the Archbishopric of
Canterbury, and by the end of the 7th century his mission had
succeeded. Then came the Danes, destroying towns and
villages, churches and abbeys along the coast, although the tiny
Saxon churches below the South Downs to the west largely
escaped. For four years the Saxon troops under King Alfred
waged war against them, concealing themselves in the
Andredsweald and sallying forth to strike when opportunity
arose; earthworks south of Kenardington in Romney Marsh
(Tour 5) are believed to have been built by the King as one of
his defensive positions. Then the Danes withdrew, and until
the coming of the Normans the region enjoyed a period of
peace. It was during these years that settlements began to
spring up inside the Weald, although human habitation continued to be mainly outside or on the fringe of the forest.

What little remains above ground of the Saxon occupation
of Kent and Sussex has been incorporated into later buildings,
mainly in the churches and abbeys. Yet many of the villages

date from the era, as their names suggest. 'Den' was the Saxon word for an enclosed space, and in the Kentish Weald there are numerous towns and villages with this suffix: Tenterden, Rolvenden, Marden, Biddenden, Benenden and many others. The few 'dens' in Sussex, such as Witherenden, are found near the Kentish border, and have been replaced by other Saxon woodland words with much the same meaning. 'Ham' (Warnham, Horsham) and 'ing' (Climping, Guestling) mean a clearing; 'ley' or 'ly' (Crawley, Ardingly) a settlement, with 'ly' stressed and pronounced 'lie'. 'Hurst' is found in both counties (Goudhurst, Hawkhurst, Wadhurst, Billingshurst) and also means a clearing; so does 'stede' or 'stead'. 'Ey' is Saxon for island, such as Sheppey, meaning 'island of sheep'. 'Mer' or 'mere' indicates the presence of water. Hurstpierpoint and Herstmonceux are examples of how Saxon was later combined with Norman French. Boughton Malherbe is a further example of this combination.

The Normans

William of Normandy did not follow the pattern of earlier invaders by landing in Kent. He chose to land in Sussex, at Pevensey Bay (Tour 8), and after sacking Hastings and erecting a temporary castle there he marched inland to confront the Saxon army under Harold, marshalled on a ridge at the edge of the Weald near Battle (Tour 8). In William's view the crown of England was his by right and he had come to claim it, preferably peaceably. But Harold, who had recently defeated Harald Hadrada in Northumberland, was confident the Normans would fare no better against him and refused to abdicate. As the battle progressed it seemed at first that his confidence was justified, for the Norman losses were heavy under the accurate fire of the Kentish archers. It was Harold's death that turned the tide. Demoralized by the loss of their leader the Saxons wilted, and presently they turned and ran for the sanctuary of the Weald.

The battle won, William moved into Kent. Avoiding the Weald, he kept to the coast, and when reinforcements had arrived from Normandy he advanced on London, using the old Roman road of Watling Street. Legend has it that as his army approached Gravesend it was confronted by what appeared to be a moving forest but was in fact a Kentish army camouflaged behind leafy branches. William was given the choice of war or peace, peace being on the condition that the ancient rights and privileges of the people of Kent should be preserved. Although in no doubt of the superiority of his army, both in men and equipment, William opted for peace and promised to honour 11 the condition. But whether or not the legend is based on fact the promise was not kept. The feudal system was common on the Continent and William introduced it into England, making himself Lord Paramount. As a result the Weald ceased to be common land. It now belonged to the king and was let as fiefs to various barons and other important personages, who in turn sublet to tenants. The tenants sublet again, and this subletting continued until the common mass of the people were reduced to little more than slaves.

The Normans built fortresses at Dover and Rochester to command the Channel and the Thames Estuary. They rebuilt the cathedrals at Canterbury and Rochester and brought Lanfranc over from France to be Archbishop of Canterbury. In 1072 Canterbury was given supremacy over York, and the document recording this decision is in the cathedral archives. It bears the signatures of the two archbishops; the King, who could not write his name, signed with a cross. One hundred years later came the murder of Thomas à Becket, a deed which resulted in the cathedral becoming a Mecca for pilgrims from all over the country and started a tourist industry fostered by the towns along the various routes to the shrine, not least by Canterbury itself. Not until 350 years later, when the shrine was destroyed by order of the Crown, did the industry cease to prosper.

Canterbury Cathedral, East End

The Middle Ages and Later
Apart from a few minor skirmishes the Wars of the Roses and the Civil War of 1642 had little impact on the Southeast, but in the centuries following the Norman Conquest the region was

not without conflict. In the Barons' revolt against King John, at the beginning of the 13th century, Rochester was besieged and captured by the King, and 50 years later the Downs above Lewes were the scene of one of the bloodiest battles to be fought on English soil, when Simon de Montfort defeated Henry III.

The Peasants' Revolt of 1381, led by Wat Tyler, originated from social injustice; villeinage still existed and the peasants resented the numerous rents and fines it imposed on them. The poll tax of 1380 brought matters to a head, and insurrection broke out all over the eastern counties. Tyler's men, many armed only with pitchforks, sacked Maidstone Gaol, released the prisoners, destroyed records, and then marched on London, where they dispersed after the young King Richard met them and promised to repair their grievances. Tyler was later assassinated.

Jack Cade's rebellion in 1450, also caused by social grievances, was confined to Kent. He too marched to London, defeating the King's troops south of Sevenoaks, where a plaque commemorates the battle (Tour 6), and executed Lord Saye and Sele who, as Lord Lieutenant of Kent, was considered by the peasants to be responsible for the injustices under which they suffered. Like the Peasants' Revolt the rebellion was short-lived, and a monument near Heathfield marks where Cade was killed by a yeoman named Alexander Iden. In 1554 Sir Thomas Wyatt of Allington Castle led the men of Kent in a rebellion against Queen Mary; but after defeating the royal forces at Strood and bombarding Cooling Castle in the Hoo Peninsula he was later captured and executed.

Throughout the 14th and 15th centuries French pirates harried the Cinque Ports along the south coast, sacking and burning. When Napoleon massed his troops across the Channel at the end of the 18th century, Martello Towers and the Royal Military Canal on Romney Marsh were constructed to counter the threat of invasion. In 1939 this threat was renewed and blockhouses and tank traps were constructed inland and along the coast. Although Zeppelins had dropped a few harmless bombs on the Southeast during the First World War it was not until 1940 that the region experienced the real horrors of aerial warfare. Between 1940 and 1944 the towns and villages of Kent and Sussex were constantly bombarded from the air, with casualties to both life and property. Miraculously, however, damage to ancient and historic buildings was rare.

Industry

Travelling around the Southeast today it is difficult to recognize that in Elizabethan times it was the industrial heart of England. In the beginning the Andresweald was the home of the wild boar, which fed on the mast from the trees. As settlements sprang up on its borders the swineherds started to take their domestic pigs into the forest to feed, at first letting them roam at will and later, as the herds grew in size and penetration into the forest became deeper, making clearings and erecting enclosures in which to pen them. In time the enclosures grew into settlements and the settlements into villages, the wood from the clearings being used as building material or fuel. It was not until the 14th century, however, when Flemish weavers were brought over by Edward III to start a cloth industry, that the villages grew into small towns and the Weald became at all prosperous – not only to the cloth manufacturers, but to the sheep farmers who supplied the wool and to the men who mined the fullers earth, the special clay abundant locally, which is necessary for cleaning and drying the cloth. Kent broadcloth, made in a variety of exciting colours, became famous; but no Flemish weavers were settled in Sussex, and for a while Sussex lagged behind Kent in the growth of prosperity.

From Roman times it had been known that there was iron in the Weald. There were Roman mines in the Hastings area and at Chiddingly; but the Romans used foot-blasts to smelt the ore and the results were poor, with only a small proportion of the iron being extracted. The introduction of water power changed that. There was an abundance of wood for the furnaces, and by the end of the 16th century the Weald had become the Black Country of the South, albeit on a smaller scale, with Cranbrook (Tour 4) the biggest of the industrial towns.

As the forest dwindled new roads were built, felling yet more trees, so that communication over the region became easier. But the life of a blast-furnace lasted only as long as the surrounding supply of fuel, and it was uneconomic to bring this from a distance, so as one furnace finished another started, always further into the forest. Both Henry VIII, mindful of the needs of his navy, and Elizabeth I had foreseen the danger that the wood must eventually run out and had introduced Acts to prevent it. The felling continued, however, and by the 18th century the royal foresight had been justified.

Now the advantage was with Sussex. Not only was the Sussex Weald more extensive, but the settlements in it were fewer, leaving more wood for the furnaces. Iron was still being worked in Sussex long after the industry had ceased in Kent, although it was very much a cottage industry, with furnaces roughly made and easily demolished. It was not until 1828 that the last furnace in the Southeast, at Ashburnham, west of Battle, finally closed.

This was also the time when huge coalfields had been opened in the North and Midlands, and coal was cheaper than charcoal. The Industrial North had taken over, and steam was supplanting water and manpower as the main source of energy. Yet traces of the Wealden industry remain: in the red discolouring of small streams, in iron slag on cottage paths or less frequented lanes, in the numerous Cinder Hills and Furnace Lanes and Hammer Ponds to be found in both counties.

If the Southeast can be said to have an industrial area today then, apart from the atomic power station at Dungeness and the coalmines around Aylesham, Eythorne and Bettishanger west of Deal, it is confined to the north of the M2, which not only carries traffic to and from the Continent but is also the industrial highway of Kent. Sheerness has its steel works and its dockyards, and there are more dockyards at Chatham. There is a large oil refinery on the Isle of Grain and cement works on the estuaries of the Thames and the Medway. Paper has been made at Dartford since the 16th century, and there are further huge paper mills at Kemsley north of Sittingbourne and at Aylesford (Tour 3) north of Maidstone. But the big firms do not monopolize the paper industry in Kent, for along the rivers there are many smaller mills which continue to make paper by traditional methods.

Wealden clay is particularly suited to the making of bricks and pottery, and Wealden sand to the making of glass. London 'stocks', yellow and purple bricks made from clay found in the area around Sittingbourne and Faversham, have been used in London for 200 years, and stone roofing slates have been quarried in the Weald even longer. Dicker pottery from the area east of Lewes is famous; but in general potteries, although numerous, tend to flourish briefly and then die out. Glass has been made in Hastings for over a hundred years; near Hastings, too, are gypsum mines, known locally as 'Egyptian' mines. As is to be expected in hop-growing country there are several breweries, with Maidstone at the centre of the industry. The numerous coastal resorts are geared to the needs of the summer visitor, but it is on farming of one sort or another that the working population of the Weald and the marshlands depends largely for a living.

Architecture and Building
Although the villages of Kent and Sussex are renowned for their picturesque charm and fine state of preservation, in the   15

16th century the majority of the smaller houses were little more than hovels, as a visit to the Singleton Museum north of Chichester (Tour 12) would show. Yet despite the lack of home comfort the villager seldom left his village, working long hard hours on the land with little time or opportunity for relaxation or travel. Around the turn of the present century, however, his circumstances started to improve. Power lines brought easy warmth and light to replace the oil lamp and the coal- or wood-burning stove; an increasing use of machinery on the land lightened his workload and provided more time for leisure; buses and then cars allowed greater freedom of movement and brought London and the big towns within easy reach. Most villages now have their cluster of modern council houses, generally planned to avoid impinging too harshly on the old centre, and in most instances the cottager has preferred them to his former uncomfortable home, no matter how picturesque, with its draughts and damp, its small windows, low beams and general lack of amenities. The picturesque cottages have been left to be bought and occupied by those with the means and the will to restore and improve them. If this has occasionally caused resentment it has also played a small part in the Weald being recognized as one of the five highest priority areas of outstanding beauty in the whole of England.

The church, the manor house and the inn, grouped around the green with sometimes a pond for good measure, are the main ingredients of a typical village centre. In many villages, however, the church stands some distance apart. This was the result of the Black Death, which ravaged the country in the mid 14th century; to eradicate the plague whole villages were destroyed and rebuilt on fresh ground. But the parish churches remained intact, and they can be as beautiful and have as fascinating a history as the great cathedrals. Most of them date back to Saxon times and, although no complete Saxon building remains, portions of their later stonework are reasonably plentiful. Norman churches, massive and more solid, have fared better.

Materials used for domestic building purposes depended largely, although not entirely, on what was available locally. Because of the cost and difficulty of transport, the further back in history one goes the greater this is true of the cottages and farmhouses. On the other hand, choice of materials for the large Georgian and Victorian mansions was dictated more by fashion than by economics. The complicated geology of the Southeast has resulted in its buildings varying considerably in detail, and Kent is particularly rich in domestic buildings of most periods and styles. A wealth of timber was available in the

Priest's House, West Hoathly (see page 91)

Weald, and great wooden barns are a feature of many of the farms; and with the clay soil ideal for brick, timber and brick houses abound, the best examples being the late-medieval yeomen's hall-houses. The origin of the hall-house dates from Saxon times, when it comprised one huge room in which the whole family lived and slept. Separate kitchens and upper rooms developed later, so that the building now consisted of a central hall reaching to the roof and flanked by two two-storeyed elements, the upper storey protruding over the lower and covered by a hipped roof of plain tiles. Later still, to suit modern requirements, an upper storey was built over the hall.

With early Tudor houses the oak uprights were so close together that the width of the brick and plaster spaces between them was little more than the width of the timbers, but as inroads into the forest increased and the amount of available timber declined the uprights spread further and further apart until by the 17th and 18th centuries they became merely a frame round the brickwork. But brick and plaster was not completely weather-proof, and it became fashionable to cover all or some of the walls with hung tiles. More usual still was to use hung tiles only on the upper storey, with the ground floor of brick or stone or a mixture of both, the stone coming from the greensand ridge that separates the Weald from the Downs.

By the 18th century a popular alternative to hung-tiles cladding was weather-boarding, made from imported soft-wood; this can be seen all over Kent and to a lesser extent in East Sussex. Houses built entirely of timber were weather-proofed from top to bottom, but where the ground floor was of brick or stone only the upper storey was weather-boarded. The

17

boards are often painted white, with contrasting black window frames. In stone buildings the joints between stones are sometimes decorated with chips of Kentish ragstone, which has been quarried in the Maidstone area since Saxon times. But ragstone is hard to work and was generally used for rubble walling, particularly in churches. In general the plain tile, both as roofing and cladding, is the most common domestic building material to be seen in the Weald; slightly curved, the older tiles distorted in firing, they provide a rich variety of colour and shade.

Houses by the Medway, Aylesford

Outside the Weald brick and flint predominate, the flint being faced with brickwork at the corners. Roofs are of tile or slate and occasionally of thatch, with thatch more common in Sussex than in Kent. There are some fine brick houses in the area east of Canterbury, and 18th-century houses near the coast were often built of flint pebbles, the pebbles carefully matched in size and laid in rows, sometimes tarred or painted. In general, however the cottages and farmhouses outside the Weald are less attractive than those within. Development of the Downs did not really take off until late in the 18th century, and even today the roads that cross the South Downs are relatively few in number.

Places of Interest

The following pages contain information about things to see and places to visit in this part of Britain. You will come across many of them in the Tours. Such places have the number of the Tour printed after the county abbreviation, for example:
Headcorn, *Kent,* (Tour 4)
In most cases information is given only about places which can be visited, though occasionally a brief note has been added in order to satisfy the curiosity about an obvious landmark to which there may be no public access.

An asterisk* either before the place name itself or before the name of a building within the text means that the times of opening have been indicated in the list on page 124. The letters (NT) mean National Trust Property.

Aldington, *Kent,* (Tour 2) is a scattered village set on rising ground, and providing a fine view across Romney Marsh. Aldington Knoll was the site of a Roman beacon, and a number of Roman remains have been found in the area. The church, restored in 1875, is magnificent both inside and out, with an embattled 16th-century tower and an elaborately decorated doorway. Erasmus, the great Dutch scholar, was rector here for a year in the 16th century. It was at Aldington that Elizabeth Barton, the 'Holy Maid of Kent', suffered from fits while working as a servant in the Archbishop's house. During these fits she was given to prophesying; one prophesy led to her death, for she foretold that if Henry VIII divorced Catherine of Aragon he would lose the throne. This was adjudged to be treason, and she was executed at Tyburn.

Clergy House, Alfriston

Alfriston, *E Sx,* (Tour 9) is a large and beautiful downland village. Among its many attractive buildings is the half-   19

timbered and thatched Clergy House (NT), a pre-Reformation
parish Priest's house. But for many visitors to Alfriston the
attractions are modern – a zoo and pleasure gardens, a
children's railway, curio shops and tea rooms – with the result
that in summer traffic is very heavy.

Alkham, *Kent.* Four miles west of Dover on the B2060, this
small village lies in a sheltered valley, with the ruins of St
Radegund's Abbey on a hilltop to the east. Founded by French
monks at the end of the 12th century, the abbey was dedicated
to a German princess who had been forcibly married to a
Frankish king, and who later became a nun and founded an
abbey at Poitiers. Much of the stone from St Radegund's
Abbey was used to build Sandgate Castle, west of Folkestone;
but the gatehouse remains and the refectory is now part of a
farmhouse.

Allington Castle, *Kent,* a Carmelite retreat since 1951, stands
on a bend in the Medway north of Maidstone. A 13th-century
fortified manor house, with thick stone walls and battlemented
towers, it is surrounded by tree-girt lawns. In the 15th century it
was bought and restored by the Wyatt family, who added the
Long Gallery. The castle fell into disrepair with the death of Sir
Thomas Wyatt, who was executed in 1554 for leading a Kentish
revolt against Queen Mary. Its present perfection is due to
Lord Conway, who bought it at the beginning of this century
and spent vast sums on its restoration. The castle is open daily.

Amberley, *W Sx,* (Tour 11) is considered by some to be the
loveliest village in Sussex. Beyond the church, built around
1100 to replace the original wooden Saxon church of 670, are
the remains of the castle, a manor house built by Ralph Neville,
Bishop of Chichester, as a summer retreat and fortified in the
14th century. Past the castle are the river and the water
meadows. Amberley is accustomed to visitors, for apart from
the sightseers, artists come to paint it and anglers to fish for
trout in the Arun. Edward Stott, who spent the last 33 years of
his life in the village, regularly exhibited paintings of Amberley
at the Royal Academy, and after his death his studio became a
museum. Opposite Amberley station is the *Chalk Pits
Museum, consisting of 36 acres devoted to exhibitions of
industrial history.

Appledore, *Kent,* 6 miles southeast of Tenterden on the B2080,
is on the edge of Romney Marsh. Now 9 miles from the sea,
20   there were busy shipyards in Appledore until the great storm of

1287 changed the course of the river. It was captured by the Danes in the 9th century and sacked by the French 500 years later. Now it is a quiet place, with the church, the Red Lion and Swan hotels and the old forge forming a picturesque group at the northern end of the wide main street. Hallhouse Farm (NT), is a late 15th-century yeoman's house.

Ardingly, *W Sx,* (Tour 10). The village church is out on the Balcombe road and contains brasses to the Culpeper family, who lived at Wakehurst Place (see below). Viscountess Wolseley, an authority on Sussex, lived in Ardingly at a house she designed and built herself, naming it Culpeper; the village sign bears her arms on one side and that of the Culpeper family on the other. Ardingly College, down a road to the west, is one of the Woodward public schools; a large, red-brick building with an imposing chapel and beautiful country beyond. Just north of the village are the fields which now form the permanent home of the South of England Show, held annually in June.

*Arundel, *W Sx,* (Tour 11) is a romantic place, with its old houses and steep alleys, the stone bridge over the Arun, the little boats on the river, and rising above the trees, the battlemented towers of the castle and the vast 19th-century Catholic cathedral on the summit of the hill. The castle was begun towards the end of the 11th century, built by Roger de Montgomery, but much of it was added later, some of it as late as the 19th century. In 1138 it came into the possession of the Earls of Arundel, and it was not until the mid 16th century that it became the family seat of the Howards – Dukes of Norfolk, Earls Marshal and the premier peers of England.

The vast Barons' Hall, the walls hung with tapestries and portraits, is one of the rooms shown to the public. So is the picture gallery, which runs the width of the castle and is monopolized by family portraits. Among smaller rooms on view is the Eastern Drawing Room, in which there are the ceremonial robes of the Norfolks and relics of Mary Queen of Scots. The Fitzalan chapel (Fitzalan was the family name of the Arundels) is part of the parish church, so that Catholics and Protestants worship together under the same roof, separated by a screen. The chapel dates from the 14th century, and although it was largely destroyed by Cromwell's troops when they occupied the castle, it was restored in 1866. Arundels and Norfolks are buried here, their tombs and effigies being much in evidence. To the north of the town is Arundel Park, where a by-road to South Stoke passes Swanbourne Lake, a beauty spot favoured by picnickers. This vantage point provides also a superb view of the town of Arundel.

Ashburnham Park, *E Sx,* lies 3 miles west of Battle and was designed by Capability Brown, with an area of trees sloping down to a chain of lakes. The house, Ashburnham Place, is used as a Christian conference centre. Along the road that runs round the back of the park is Ashburnham Forge where, at the beginning of the 19th century, its closure marked the end of the Sussex iron industry.

Ashdown Forest, *E Sx,* (Tours 7 & 9) consists of 14 000 acres of heather, gorse and bracken broken by large woods. Roughly triangular in shape, it stretches from Forest Row at its apex to the line of the A26 between Crowborough and Maresfield. The highest point is Camp Hill, at 650 feet; nearby is the Diplomatic Wireless Service Station, its aerials a landmark for miles around. In the past there was constant conflict between the rights of the commoner to graze their animals and collect wood and peat, and the desire of the great lords to enclose it for their own use. John of Gaunt fenced it in to form a deer preserve. There are still deer in the forest, although they are seldom seen.

Ashford, *Kent,* is 14 miles from Canterbury on the A28, with a population of 36 000 that is rapidly expanding. The hub of five main roads, it sees plenty of traffic, although the A20 now bypasses it. The old part of the town is pleasant, with some good Georgian buildings. The Church of St Mary the Virgin has a central tower soaring to 120 feet, with 4 corner turrets; inside are several enormous tombs, including that of Sir John Fogge, who financed rebuilding work in the 15th century. Although Ashford is an excellent shopping centre, with good residential areas and a large girls' school, since the 19th century it has grown in importance as a railway town. It is at the junction of several lines and contains the main BR construction and maintenance works for rolling stock.

Ashurst, *W Sx,* (Tour 10). The main attraction is the small flint church, built at the end of the 12th century by the Knights Templar during the Transitional period; the nave and aisle occupy a single space, the rest of the building being the base of the tower. A horn above the north door was used to keep the congregation in tune, as at Charing (see below).

Aylesford, *Kent,* (Tour 3) is one of the most photographed villages in the county, with its old buildings grouped round the medieval bridge. It has a long history. Prehistoric monuments on the Downs suggest it was a settlement long before the Romans came, and Bronze and Iron Age remains have been found in the area. Horsa was killed here in battle against the Britons in the 5th century.

Although the area is now largely industrial, with the vast Reed Paper Works and modern housing estates, the village still manages to retain its picturesque charm.

It was in Aylesford in the 13th century that the Carmelites (later to be expelled by Cromwell) established the Friars, the first priory in England.

The Friars was owned for a short while by the Wyatts (see Allington Castle) and early in the 17th century it came into the possession of Sir John Banks, whose huge memorial is in Aylesford church. Sir John did much to improve the priory, but it is the Carmelites, who returned in 1949, to whom most of the credit is due for its rebuilding. The original gatehouse and cloisters remain, the galleries have been added to the hall. The Friars is now a shrine for pilgrims.

Balcombe, *W Sx,* (Tour 10) is on the edge of Balcombe Forest. The church, high above the road, dates from Norman times, the 18th-century Balcombe House being the original parsonage. South towards Haywards Heath is the 1500-foot long Balcombe viaduct, built around 1840, that carries the railway over the Ouse – here only a stream. North of the village is Highley Manor; set in 7½ acres of grounds it was built in the 14th century for the Duke of Norfolk. Later it became the property of Elizabeth I, and in 1669 it was bought by the Shelley family. The poet, Percy Bysshe Shelley, lived at Highley. It was demolished in 1880 and rebuilt as a replica of the original house. In 1980 it was opened as a hotel.

*****Battle,** *E Sx,* (Tour 8) is an attractive town and the scene of the Battle of Hastings. This was a battle the Saxons should have won, for they had ground advantage; but with Harold's death his army lost heart and melted away, to be butchered whenever and wherever they were caught. William founded the Abbey of St Martin to commemorate his victory, siting the High Altar on the spot where Harold fell. What now remains is of later date, and the Great Gatehouse that dominates the market square was built early in the 14th century. The abbey was largely demolished at the time of the Dissolution, but much remains, including the monks' common rooms and sleeping quarters.   23

The abbot's house, altered and enlarged over the years, is now a girls' school.

Near the Abbey gates is the Pilgrims' Rest, a 15th-century timbered house standing back from the square. The 12th-century parish church of St Mary's has a 15th-century tower; in the sanctuary is the tomb of Sir Anthony Browne, Master of the King's Horse, who was largely responsible for the destruction of the abbey. Langton House Museum contains a diorama of the Battle of Hastings and a reproduction of the Bayeux Tapestry.

*__Bayham Abbey,__ *E Sx,* (Tour 7) has recently been restored. It is a noble ruin on the banks of the Teise, and dates from the 13th century. Much of the Great Church and the gatehouse has survived. Across the river, which forms the boundary between Kent and East Sussex, is the new abbey.

__Bedgebury Forest,__ *Kent,* (Tour 4). Part of the 2000 acres is run by the Forestry Commission as a National Pinetum and maintained as an experimental area for raising, among others, conifers and deciduous trees. Between the trees are broad avenues along which visitors may walk. The pinetum is always open, and there is a large car-park.

*__Bentley Wildfowl Gardens,__ *E Sx,* are 3 miles south of Uckfield near the village of Halland. In the 25-acre grounds, complete with ponds, more than 100 varieties of wildfowl live in as near natural conditions as man can contrive. The house is a 1960 Palladian style conversion of a Tudor farmhouse.

__Berwick,__ *E Sx,* an isolated village eight miles east of Lewes, is notable for the church murals. These were done by local artists, among them Vanessa and Quentin Bell, and were commissioned by the Bishop of Chichester in 1941. They depict local people and scenes in religious settings.

__Bethersden,__ *Kent,* (Tour 4), is a typical Wealden village, with weather-boarded houses and a Perpendicular church. Stone mined near here during the Middle Ages, known as Bethersden marble, was used in many churches and cathedrals, including Canterbury and Rochester, as well as for flooring and street paving.

__Bexhill,__ *E Sx,* is a seaside town between Eastbourne and Hastings, with a population of around 35 000. One of the last of the coastal villages to follow Brighton's example, it did not develop as a holiday resort until the mid 19th century, when Lord de la Warr began building on land between the old town and the sea. It still has some way to go to catch up on its neighbours; it has, for instance, no pier. Its main attraction is the de la Warr pavilion, with the Marine Arcade and Marine Court Avenue beside it. Old Bexhill is inland. At its centre is St Peter's church, dating from 1070 with traces of Saxon origin. Opposite the church are the ruins of the old manor house.

Biddenden, *Kent,* (Tour 4) is very much a tourist attraction, with its share of antique shops, tea-shops and pubs. Among the many lovely half-timbered houses is the Old Cloth Hall north of the green, with its gables and black-and-white timberwork. The church is 13th century, made of Bethersden marble, as are the paving slabs in the main street. Biddenden is famous for its Siamese twins, Eliza and Mary Chulkhurst, joined at hip and shoulder. They were born early in the 12th century and died, aged 34, within a few hours of each other after bequeathing money to be used in the distribution of Easter cakes, stamped with their image, to the village poor.

***Bignor Roman Villa,** *W Sx,* (Tour 12), was discovered in 1811 and is one of the largest in the country, with a museum displaying items of interest found on the site. The North corridor, which is covered, is 80 feet long and contains some fine mosaics.

Mosaic Pavement, Roman Villa, Bignor

Billingshurst, *W Sx,* is a large village at the junction of the A272 and the A29 – the Pilgrims' Way and the Roman Stane Street. The church, which stands high above a small, sloping green, has a 15th-century wooden ceiling and a fine Tudor porch below the tower. In general, however, the village gives an impression of modernity rather than of age.

Bilsington, *Kent,* (Tour 5) is a hillside village on the edge of Romney Marsh. North of the village are the remains of Bilsington Priory, founded in 1253, where the Archibishops of Canterbury stayed when visiting the Marsh; the later priory which adjoins it is now a private home. Near the 13th-century church is a 52-foot obelisk, erected in 1835 as a memorial to Sir William Conway, who at one time owned the priory and was killed when his coach overturned. Left of the church is the cliff which marked the coastline before the sea receded.

Birchington, *Kent,* is a seaside resort on the north coast of the Isle of Thanet. In the medieval All Saints Church are a number of memorials to the Crispe family, who lived at Quex Park, and a window in memory of Dante Gabriel Rossetti, who died at Birchington in 1882 and whose grave in the churchyard is marked with a Celtic cross. In Quex Park is the Powell-Cotton Big Game Museum, with stuffed animals exhibited in their natural habitats together with a fine collection of primitive weapons, costumes and musical instruments. Nearby is RAF Manston, a Battle of Britain aerodrome, with a small number of aircraft on display.

Birling Gap, *E Sx,* is a break in the cliffs between Eastbourne and Seaford, favoured by smugglers in the past and the starting point for a splendid 2½-mile walk over the top of the Seven Sisters to Cuckmere Haven. This is a dangerous part of the coast; the shore line is a mass of huge boulders on which the sea breaks thunderously, and many a ship has foundered here. The Belle Tout lighthouse that guarded it was replaced by one at Beachy Head, and is now a private house.

Bishopsbourne, *Kent,* (Tour 2), is a small woodland village. The church is long and narrow, with stained glass by Burne-Jones and containing a bust of Richard Hooker, an expert on ecclesiastical constitution and rector of Bishopsbourne for several years. Joseph Conrad lived here, spending the last years of his life at 'Oswalds', the present rectory. North of the village is Bourne House, one of the finest Queen Anne houses in Kent, with a lovely park.

Black Down, *W Sx,* (Tour 12), at 919 feet, is the highest point in Sussex. The National Trust owns much of the area, including Tennyson's Lane, where the poet built Aldworth House. He lived here for the last 20 years of his life, writing *Idylls of The King* and other poems.

Blean, *Kent,* (Tour 1). Blean Woods are remnants of the old royal Forest of Blean and are protected by the Nature Conservancy because of their wealth of animal and plant life. North of Blean is Honey Hill, from which there is a magnificent view southward.

Bluebell Line, *Sx,* (Tour 9) is a five-mile stretch of railway linking Horsted Keynes with Sheffield Park. The line is so named because in spring the woodland bordering the track is a mass of bluebells. Originally part of the old East Grinstead to Lewes railway, in 1960 it was taken over and is run by a group of enthusiasts, with numerous engines and carriages bought from other railways and restored to their original colours. There are buffets at the termini, and it is interesting to walk round the yards and inspect the rolling stock. The Bluebell Line has been a boon to film makers wishing to depict journeys of the past in a steam locomotive. Horsted Keynes village is over a mile from the station, which is one reason why BR could not make it pay.

Bodiam Castle

*****Bodiam Castle,** *E Sx,* (Tour 8), (NT). One of the best-preserved examples of medieval architecture, it was built by Sir Edward Dalyngrigge to guard an important crossing of the River Rother which was left vulnerable after Rye and Winchelsea had been sacked by the French. By the time the castle was completed, however, in 1388, the threat of invasion was past, so that its defences were never tested and the grandeur and symmetry of its outer walls and towers remain unimpaired. Rectangular in shape, and measuring 150 feet by 135 feet overall, the castle is contained by massive curtain walls 41 feet high, with 60-foot drum towers at the corners and a square tower in each of the east and west walls. Much of the interior was destroyed by Roundheads during the Civil War, but enough remains to see the layout of the rooms, ranged round a central courtyard and planned to combine comfort with defence. Lord Curzon, who bought the castle in 1916 and

27

bequeathed it to the National Trust in 1926, described it as 'the most romantic and fairy of English castles'.

Bognor Regis, *W Sx,* is a cheerful seaside resort 7 miles west of Littlehampton, its seafront short in comparison with most of its competitors. Queen Victoria called it 'dear little Bognor', whereas George V's comment was less complimentary (see Pagham). There are some good 19th-century houses, including the Royal Norfolk Hotel; the impressive new Regis Centre was opened in 1980. Hotham Park, with its Arboretum and children's zoo, is named after Sir Richard Hotham, a wealthy Londoner who bought land in the area at the end of the 18th century with a view to profitable development.

Bonnington, *Kent,* 7 miles west of Hythe and just north of the B2067, is an old-established settlement. Sailing barges from Rye once brought coal up the Rother here. Its parish church is the oldest on the Marsh and is dedicated to St Rumwold, who was born able to talk and preached a sermon before dying when he was only three days old! (See Boxley).

Bosham, *W Sx,* (Tour 12), pronounced 'Bozzam', is a boating centre on Chichester Harbour and one of the beauty spots of the Sussex coast. There are some attractive brick-and-flint houses, and a small arcade where local craftsmen can be seen at work. Both the Emperor Vespasian and King Canute are believed to have lived here. Earl Godwin and his son Harold certainly did, for the Bayeux tapestry depicts Harold praying in Bosham church before sailing to Normandy to negotiate with William. The lovely 11th-century church was probably built on the site of a former Saxon monastery – by Canute, if legend is correct. His daughter was almost certainly buried here; a stone coffin containing the remains of a young child and dating from the 11th century was found in 1865. A second coffin, containing bones believed to be those of Earl Godwin, was found some years later.

*Boughton Place, *Kent,* (Tour 3) is reached through an avenue of trees from Boughton Green. It is a gabled Elizabethan mansion, built by Robert Rudstone; the broad staircase was added later, as were the pillars in the hall. The house contains some fine furniture and several good portraits; there is also a costume museum on the first floor and a collection of carriages in the stables. Boughton church has the best medieval lych-gate in Kent, and from the lovely churchyard there is a fine view to the Wealden hills.

Boxley, *Kent,* (Tour 3) is an attractive little village at the foot of the Downs, with the church at the centre and Boxley Park adjacent to it. Boxley Abbey, at Abbey Gate, is now a ruin apart from a large 13th-century stone barn. The abbey was founded by the Cistercians in the 12th century and was famous for two apparently miraculous images. One was a jointed figure of Christ on the cross which could be cunningly manipulated. The other was a statue of St Rumwold (see also Bonnington), held to the ground by a concealed pin. If the pilgrim gave generously a monk would surreptitiously remove the pin so that the statue could be lifted; otherwise it remained immovable. The abbey was dissolved in the 16th century.

Bramber, *W Sx,* (Tour 10). A historic village, like its neighbour Steyning it was an important port before the Adur silted up in the 14th century; both King John and Edward I are known to have visited Bramber, and the Knights Templar had a house here. Bramber Castle, with the 76-foot tower-keep and part of its outer walls remaining, stands on a hill north of the main road. Built at the time of the Conquest on the site of an old Saxon fortification, for 600 years it was owned by the Dukes of Norfolk, but is now part of the National Trust. Adjacent to the castle is the parish church of St Nicholas, originally the castle chapel and believed to be not only the first Norman church to be built in Sussex, but also the only church in England to have its chancel in the tower. Both castle and church suffered damage at the hands of Cromwell's troops.

At the other end of the village is the timber-framed house of St Mary's, home of a butterfly collection and the oldest medieval domestic building in Sussex. It was built in the 15th century for the monks in charge of the chapel that stood on a now vanished bridge across the Adur. Charles II is reputed to have stayed in St Mary's before escaping to France after the Battle of Worcester. A few doors away, opposite the car-park, is the 'House of Pipes' containing 25 000 objects connected with smoking, from cigarette cards to opium pipes.

Brede, *E Sx,* is a small village overlooking the river, 6 miles north of Hastings on the A28. The church is 12th century with a 16th-century tower. In the south chapel is the tomb of Sir Goddard Oxenbridge, who lived at Brede Place and was reputed to be a child-eater. As Sir Goddard was a pious man, this seems unlikely. But according to the story the children retaliated by getting him drunk and then sawing him in half. Brede Place is a small brick and stone house overlooking the river valley, and one of the oldest in the village. Built by Sir

Thomas Ford (its original name was Ford Place) in the 14th century, it was sold to the Oxenbridge family in 1619, and they in turn sold it to the Frewens (see Northiam). The house is reputed to be haunted.

Brenchley, *Kent,* (Tour 4) is a peaceful, wooded village on a hillside, far removed from traffic. Many of the buildings around the green are of architectural or historic interest. On a hill northeast of the village a double ring of earthworks marks the site where Knowle Castle once stood.

Brightling, *E Sx,* (Tour 8). The village is famous as the home of Squire Jack Fuller, known as 'Mad Jack' or 'Honest Jack', who lived at Rose Hill, now Brightling Park. Fuller was one of Sussex's most eccentric characters. He once wagered a friend that from his house he could see the spire of Dallington church, 2 miles to the southwest; discovering he was wrong, he built an imitation spire where, as seen from the house, it could be mistaken for the real thing. The folly is still there, at Wood's Corner. Fuller was a patron of Turner, gave liberally to charity, and was twice a member of Parliament. He was also interested in science, building a hill-top observatory that is still in use near the village. Among his other constructions were an obelisk on the Brightling Downs and a triangular mausoleum in the churchyard where, on his death in 1834, he was buried. It is reputed that his body was bound by iron chains – which, if true, seems appropriate, for the Fuller fortune was founded on iron.

Royal Pavilion, Brighton

Brighton, *E Sx,* (Tour 10). Originally Brighthelmstone, a small
fishing village within the area of alleyways and shops now

known as The Lanes, it is the largest town in the Southeast with a resident population of around 166 000. The transformation began in 1750, when a Dr Richard Russell published a treatise entitled *A Dissertation Concerning the Use of Sea Water in Diseases of the Glands*. The 'use' became popular, and the seaside holiday – and Brighton – were born. They came to maturity with the visit of the Prince Regent in 1783 and the building of his Royal Pavilion 4 years later.

The first pavilion was relatively simple, but the Prince wanted something more sumptuous and exotic. The present pavilion, with its domes and minarets and its Oriental interior, was built by John Nash early in the 19th century. On the ground floor is the Banqueting Room with its glittering chandeliers, the Music Room, the vast kitchen full of gleaming copper pots and pans, and the two drawing rooms separated by a circular salon. The King's apartments are also on the ground floor; the bedrooms of Queen Victoria and Princess Charlotte are upstairs. Tall windows overlook a green square, where the old outbuildings have been put to other uses, including an Art Gallery and Museum and the Dome Concert Hall.

Part of Brighton's attraction lies in its fine squares and crescents and their elegant houses, now largely converted into flats or small hotels. In the churchyard of the old parish church of St Nicholas in Dyke Road, with its intricately carved Norman font, is the grave of Phoebe Hessel, who lived to be 108 after being wounded at Fontenoy while serving in the army as a private; the present parish church of St Peter's, built in 1820, stands on an island at the junction of the roads to London and Lewes, an imposing building in an imposing position. Even more imposing is St Bartholomew's in Ann Street, built of brick with a nave over 130 feet high.

There are several museums and many lovely parks, with some fine floral displays. The big hotels are mainly along the front, where a conference centre was opened in 1976. Opposite the Palace Pier is the famous Aquarium and its Dolphinarium, and eastward is the elegant arcade of Madiera Drive and Volk's Electric Railway, the latter opened in 1883, the first in Britain. Further east still is the new Brighton Marina, second largest in the world, its 900 moorings already fully booked.

Broadstairs, *Kent,* is a seaside resort on the Isle of Thanet with some fine hotels and an excellent sandy beach. Queen Victoria used to stay here, and Charles Dickens, who loved the town, lived and wrote at Bleak House, now a Dickens museum. The steep Harbour Street, with the 16th-century York Gate at the bottom, is most attractive. So is the harbour, and the weather-boarded harbourmaster's office. The inland village of St Peter's, with open country beyond, has a splendid 12th-century church. North of Broadstairs is the North Foreland Lighthouse. (See Margate).

Brookland, *Kent,* is a marsh village 6 miles northeast of Rye on the A259. The tower of the beautiful St Augustine's church is detached from the main building; legend has it that at one time so many villagers were living together out of wedlock that when a young couple did apply to be married the church was so startled that the belfry fell off. Inside the church is a circular font displaying the signs of the Zodiac, and part of a wall – painting depicting the murder of Thomas à Becket.

Burpham, *W Sx,* (Tour 11) is one of the loveliest of Sussex villages, remote from major roads. The Arun flows nearby, and from the green one can gaze across to Arundel. Flint and thatch are prominent, and part of the flint walls of the church goes back to pre-Conquest days.

Burwash, *E Sx,* (Tour 8). Standing high in wooded country, Burwash is a picturesque village, and even before Kipling's arrival visitors came to enjoy its charm. In the 11th-century church there is a tablet to Kipling's son John, who was killed at Loos in 1915, and his name is on the war memorial, which Kipling unveiled. In the churchyard is the oldest known Sussex iron grave-slab.
*Batemans. This was the home of Rudyard Kipling from 1902 until his death in 1936. It was built in 1634 and has been described as the loveliest small house in Sussex. It was here that he wrote *Puck of Pook's Hill* and many of his Sussex poems; here too he wrote his autobiography, *Something of Myself,*

Batemans, Burwash

finishing it three weeks before he died. His study, with all the paraphernalia of the writer, is much as he left it; on the walls are plaques carved by his sculptor father and used as illustrations for his books. The garden, largely planned by Kipling himself, leads down to the Dudwell, where there is a recently restored watermill, which he used to generate electricity. The house was acquired by the National Trust in 1940, under the will of Mrs Kipling.

Bury, *W Sx,* is on the A29, 2 miles north of Arundel Park. From Bury Hill there is a fine view of the village, with the main street leading off to the church and the river, the houses surrounded by trees and bushes. Bury House, once the home of John Galsworthy, stands by the crossroads and is now an old people's home. From the 13th-century church there is a pleasant walk down a footpath to the Arun, with a view of the Downs across the river.

Buxted, *E Sx,* (Tour 9). Although the village was originally situated in Buxted Park, in the 19th century the owner, Lord Liverpool, decided he wanted the place to himself. So by refusing to repair the cottages he forced the villagers to move out. The church, however, is still inside the park; as, incidentally, is the cricket ground. An iron slab over the doorway of a house near the park entrance bears the picture of a hog and the date 1581, the year in which the house was built by Ralph Hogge, a local iron founder and probably the first man to cast guns in England.

Camber, *E Sx,* (Tour 5) is a modern village near the border with Kent. It has an excellent sandy beach, backed by a varied collection of bungalows and caravans. Across the Rother are the remains of Camber Castle, although to reach it from Camber involves a detour of some 5 miles through Rye. Circular in shape, the castle was one of a series built by Henry VIII to guard against invasion by the French.

Canterbury, *Kent,* (Tour 1) is a cathedral city on the site of the Roman Durovernum and a Saxon stronghold. Here, in 597, St Augustine began his conversion of the English with the baptism of Ethelbert, King of Kent. In Canterbury Cathedral, in 1170, Thomas à Becket was murdered by Henry II's knights, a deed which motivated a pilgrimage that was to last until the shrine was detroyed 350 years later by order of the Crown. During the Second World War Canterbury was savagely blitzed in the

33

'Baedecker Raid' of 1942; miraculously the cathedral suffered only minor damage, most of the destruction being confined to the southeast of the city.

Within its encircling walls Canterbury is a city of narrow streets and timber-framed houses, roughly divided into four quadrants.

Canterbury Cathedral, one of the finest in Europe and seat of the Primate of All England, is in the northeast quadrant. Begun by Lanfranc in the 11th century, it was completed by Anselm, although the northwest tower was demolished and rebuilt in the 19th century. The Bell Harry Tower dominates the scene from all directions, but from the south one can admire the exquisite southeast transept and the Norman arcading of St Anselm's chapel. Entrance at the western end leads through Yvele's spacious nave, built in Chaucer's time, to William of Sens' choir. At the eastern end is the Trinity Chapel, where Becket's shrine was housed, and everywhere there are the marvellous blues and purples of the medieval stained glass. North of the cathedral proper are the monastery buildings, the cloisters and the chapter house and the 12th-century water tower. Still further north is the King's School, built by Henry VIII, with its remarkable Norman staircase leading to the school library, once a pilgrims' hall.

In the northwest quadrant is the picturesque Weavers House, where refugees from the Continent brought their skills to the city in Elizabethan times. Here too are the church dedicated to St Alphege and the remains of the 13th-century house of the Black Friars. The ruins of the Grey Friars House are in the southwest quadrant, together with the Poor Priests' Hospital, home of the Buffs military museum, and the impressive shell of Canterbury Castle. In the public gardens in the southeast quadrant is Dane John Mound, a prehistoric earthwork, and the Invicta, a George Stephenson locomotive that ran on the old Canterbury-Whitstable line.

Out on the Sandwich road are the ruins of St Augustine's Abbey, where the early archbishops were buried. The original Saxon building was replaced in the 11th century by a bigger church, which was in turn largely destroyed at the Dissolution. Northwest of the abbey is St Augustine's College, built in the 19th century as a training centre for missionaries. East of the abbey, beyond the prison, stands the oldest church in continuous use in England. This is St Martin's, where Queen Bertha worshipped before the conversion of her husband, King Ethelbert. Away on the Whitstable road is the modern

University of Kent, high on St Thomas's Hill with the attractive village of Hackington below.

Chanctonbury Ring, *W Sx,* is the most famous landmark on the South Downs; a clump of beech trees planted in 1760 by Charles Goring, who lived at Wiston, an Elizabethan mansion below the north face of the Downs. The trees are in the perimeter of an Iron Age fort, which also contains the remains of a Roman temple. At 780 feet Chanctonbury is not the highest point on the Downs, but on a clear day the view extends northward to the Surrey border and southward to the Channel. It is best reached by a lane off the A283, west of Steyning.

Charing, *Kent,* (Tour 3) is a charming little town, although partially spoilt by council-built cottages, and was probably the site of the Roman settlement of *Durolenum.* The nave and aisles of the church, like those of Ashurst in Sussex, occupy a single space; also like Ashurst, there is a vamping horn, now in the vestry, which was used for keeping the congregation in time. Down the road to the church are the remains of the Archbishop's palace; the old banqueting hall is now a barn and a Tudor farmhouse has been built among the ruins.

Chartham, *Kent,* (Tour 1). Despite the large paper-mill – paper has been made in Chartham for over 200 years – it is a pretty village, with a huge church built in the reign of Edward I and containing the oldest set of five bells in the county. One of the knights connected with its promotion, Sir Robert de Septvans, was buried in the chancel. His memorial, a magnificent brass effigy, is in the north transept.

*****Chartwell,** *Kent,* (Tour 6), (NT), the home of Sir Winston Churchill, is 2 miles south of Westerham with magnificent views over the Weald. The building itself is not outstanding, and it is its association with its former occupant that attracts the visitors. Everywhere there are reminders of him; his walking sticks in the hall, medals and photographs in the anteroom, the uniform room (Churchill loved dressing up), the study where he did much of his writing. The association continues in the garden. There are the lawns on which he strolled with his dog, the orchard he planted, the pond where he fed the goldfish, the high wall he built. And near the wall is the studio where he loved to sit and paint.

Chatham, *Kent,* at the mouth of the Medway, has so merged with Rochester and Gillingham that the boundaries are imperceptible. It is strictly a naval and military town, as it has been since Elizabethan times. Many of the great wooden ships of the line were launched here, including the *Victory*. Now the dockyard, parts of which can be visited, is mainly engaged in the building of submarines. The sail loft, built by French prisoners of war, is nearly 300 feet long, and the rope shed is even longer. Brompton Barracks, built at the beginning of the 19th century for the Royal Artillery, is now the home of the Royal School of Military Engineering and has a comprehensive museum dealing with every aspect of the Royal Engineers' specialist activities. In Chatham Town Hall is a model of the *Victory*, and a sedan chair used by the garrison commanders; the 1000-year old mayoral chain, originally worn by the Doges of Venice, can be seen on request. And Chatham, like so much of Kent, has associations with Dickens. When Dickens was a boy his father lived in Ordnance Terrace and worked in the dockyard's Navy Pay Office.

Chelwood Gate, *E Sx,* is little more than a hamlet on the A275, 6 miles south of East Grinstead. The common stretches away on either side of the main road, a spread of gorse and heather with a scheduled picnic area. Down the lane opposite the Red Lion is Birchgrove House, home of Harold Macmillan. The gardens of the house, a mixture of the formal and the natural, with a heart-shaped swimming pool, are sometimes open to the public on a Sunday afternoon in spring, when the profusion of daffodils is a delight. Where the lane meets the main road a seat commemorates the visit of John Kennedy in 1963.

Chichester, *W Sx,* (Tour 12) is a cathedral city roughly circular in shape, divided into four quadrants by the suitably named North, South, East and West Streets, which meet at the octagonal city cross, erected in 1501 and now the centre of a pedestrian precinct.

City Cross, Chichester

Chichester Cathedral, begun by Bishop de Luffa late in the 11th century, was restored and strengthened after the wooden roof had been destroyed by fire in 1187, the spire being added in the 15th century. In 1861 both tower and spire collapsed, but were rebuilt within 6 years. The beauty of the interior is enhanced by its art work. Behind the high altar is John Piper's enormous tapestry, installed in 1966, the central panels representing the Holy Trinity, the outer ones the elements and the evangelists. 12th-century stone panels in the south choir aisle depict Christ with Mary and Martha and the raising of Lazarus. In the transepts are huge portraits of royalty and clergy, painted on wood early in the 16th century, and in St Mary Magdelene's chapel there is the Graham Sutherland painting of Christ appearing to Mary after the Resurrection. Most of the memorials installed prior to the Civil War were destroyed by Cromwell's troops, but a few have survived, including the 13th-century tombs of the Earl and Countess of Arundel.

The cathedral, together with the Vicar's Hall, now a restaurant, and the Bishop's Palace are in the 3rd quadrant, between West and South Streets. Across South Street are the Pallants and the RDC offices in Pallant House. Here too is the antique market. In the 1st quadrant is St Mary's Hospital, a 13th-century infirmary converted into flats for the elderly, and Priory Park, with the motte of the old castle and a museum devoted to the history of the city. The main museum is further south. On North Street is the 18th-century Council House, containing a fine array of city treasures, and below it St Olave's, a medieval church now in use as a bookshop. North of the old city is Oaklands Park and the Festival Theatre.

Chiddingly, *E Sx,* (Tour 9). The 15th-century spire of Chiddingly church reaches a height of 130 feet and is one of the few stone spires in Sussex. Inside the church are massive monuments to the Jeffray family, who owned Chiddingly Place, a Tudor mansion of which little survives.

****Chiddingstone,** *Kent,* (Tour 7), is largely owned by the National Trust. It is one of the most beautiful villages in Kent, with the Castle Inn and a row of lovely 16th- and 17th-century timber and brick or plaster houses opposite the 14th-century sandstone church. In the church are many memorials to the Streatfield family, who lived at Chiddingstone Castle for over 400 years. The castle is an 18th-century Gothic conversion of an old manor house, set in picturesque surroundings. It houses important collections of Jacobite relics and oriental objets 37

d'art, in addition to some intereting pictures and furniture. The 3-acre lake is popular with local fishermen.

Chiddingstone Castle

*Chilham, *Kent,* (Tour 2), is one of the loveliest and most visited villages in the county. Away from main road traffic, it stands high above the Stour valley, with picturesque Jacobean and Tudor houses surrounding the square, now a car-park. At the top of the square is the castle, a brick manor house attributed to Inigo Jones and built by Sir Dudley Digges early in the 17th century on the site of a Norman castle, the keep of which is hidden by the house. Sir Dudley is buried in the church, along with members of his family. The castle, now the home of Viscount Masserene and Ferrard, is not open to the public but the gardens, attributed to Capability Brown, may be visited. There is a good view of the castle from the park, which stretches as far as Godmersham. To help with the upkeep Lord Masserene provides entertainment in the form of medieval banquets and exhibitions of jousting and falconry.

Cissbury Ring, *W Sx,* (Tour 11), (NT), is an Iron Age hill-fort 600 feet up on the Downs, with views to Beachy Head and the Isle of Wight. The fort is surrounded by a ditch and rampart and is one of the largest in the country. Inside the fort there are filled-in shafts of an early Neolithic flint-mining industry; the fort was later abandoned, although the Romans partially re-fortified it against the Saxons. Cissbury Ring is best reached by a lane from Findon.

Clayton, *E Sx,* is a tiny village situated at the junction of the A273 and B2112 under the Downs, famous for its two wind-mills known as Jack and Jill. Henry Longhurst, the golfing commentator and writer, lived in a house sandwiched between them. By the road junction is Clayton railway tunnel, the entrance a turreted brick monstrosity with a small inhabited house between the towers. Bronze Age burial relics have been found in the parish, also pieces from the tiled pavements of the

Roman road that passed through the village. The church of St John is pre-Conquest and famous for its wall paintings believed to be as old as the church and including an amazingly detailed representation of the Last Judgment.

Cliffe, *Kent,* at the end of the B2000 and the most north-westerly village on the Hoo Peninsula, was an important place in Saxon times, for it was here that churchmen met for their annual synod. Offa, King of Mercia, built a church here, the only church in Kent dedicated to St Helen. The present large church dates from the 13th century and contains a number of wall paintings. Cliffe was largely destroyed by fire in 1520, but returned to prosperity in the Victorian building boom. Near the village is an important petrol storage depot.

Cobham, *Kent,* on the B2009 3 miles west of Rochester, is an attractive village on the edge of the western Downs. The church is famous for the medieval brasses that pave the chancel, one of the finest collections in the world. On the south side of the church are the 14th-century almshouses, with the original hall and kitchen and the pensioners' rooms leading off the hall. Across the road is the timbered Leather Bottle inn, immortalized by Dickens in the *Pickwick Papers.*
Cobham Hall, one of the largest houses in Kent and now a girls' school, is a fine example of a Tudor manor house. The original house, built by the Cobhams in the 13th century, has vanished; the nucleus of the present building dates from the 16th century. Early in the 17th century ownership passed to the Stuarts, Dukes of Richmond, who built the present central block; their successors, the Earls of Darnley, completed the building as it is today. James Wyatt, and later the Reptons, were responsible for much of the work, both inside and out. The huge Gilt Hall, two storeys high, was once the banqueting hall and was later converted into a music room. On an upper floor is the magnificent Darnley stage coach, built early in the 18th century. To the east of the house is the 18th-century mausoleum, intended as the final resting place for generations of Darnleys to come but never completed (and never conse-crated) and now a ruin.
Owletts (NT), a red-brick house of Charles II's reign, lies at the western end of the village. Built by a Kent farmer it has a Caroline staircase with an ornate plasterwork ceiling and belonged to the Baker family from 1794 to 1938, when it was given to the National Trust, together with several cottages and 25 acres of garden, by Sir Herbert Baker, the architect, who continued to live there until his death in 1946.

A mile away at Sole Street is a Tudor Yeoman's house (NT), restored by Sir Herbert Baker, which can be viewed on written application to the tenant.

Coldrum Long Barrow, *Kent,* (Tour 6), (NT), is a Neolithic burial chamber dating from about 2 000BC, one of the finest on the North Downs. In 1926 the barrow was given to the National Trust as a memorial to Benjamin Harrison, the archaeologist, who died in 1921 aged 84.

Coolham, *W Sx,* is a small village 3 miles southeast of Billingshurst on the A272. Not far away, at a bend in the road, a lane leads down to an Elizabethan farmhouse, now a Quaker meeting house and guest house with the intriguing name of Blue Idol. William Penn used to walk here from his home in Warminghurst, 3 miles away across the fields to the south.

Cooling, *Kent,* is a village in the centre of the Hoo Peninsula overlooking the marshes. In the churchyard of St James are 13 small gravestones as described by Dickens in *Great Expectations.* Beyond the church is Cooling Castle, built by Lord Cobham in 1381 to defend the mouth of the Thames; Cooling Castle was the home of Sir John Oldcastle, on whom some say Shakespeare modelled Falstaff. A follower of Wycliffe, Sir John was burnt as a heretic in 1417. The fortifications of the castle were largely destroyed by the rebels under Thomas Wyatt in 1554.

Cowdray Park, *W Sx,* (Tour 12) forms the eastern approach to Midhurst. Undulating and wooded, it is an ideal place for a picnic beside the lake. There is a golf course, and probably the most famous polo ground in the country, much favoured by the Royal Family. In the southwest corner are the ruins of Cowdray House, home of the Montagues until it was destroyed by fire in 1793. The tall gatehouse still stands, and enough remains of the building to follow the original layout.

Cowfold, *W Sx,* (Tour 10). This is an attractive village with a delightful churchyard. Inside the church is a brass memorial over 40 square feet in area, the largest in the county. South of Cowfold is St Hugh's, the only Carthusian monastery in the British Isles. It is a vast place with an enormous church whose spire can be seen rising above the trees, and a cloister that encloses over three acres of orchard. The huge gatehouse reflects the desire of its inmates to remain aloof from the world, but the monastery may be visited by arrangement.

Cranbrook, *Kent,* (Tour 4), vies with Tenterden for the title 'Capital of the Weald'. Its houses are weather-boarded and tile-hung, its streets often hilly. On the corner of the High Street is the old George Hotel, where Elizabeth I once stayed. Up Stone Street is an ancient smock mill, still partly operational and probably the finest in Britain. The splendid 15th century parish church has the figure of Father Time above the tower clock; legend has it that as the vicar could not afford a gardener to scythe the churchyard grass Father Time came down at night to do it for him. Inside the church is a pit which is considered to be unique in Britain, its purpose being the total immersion of adults in baptism; and in a room over the south porch, known as 'Baker's Hole', Sir John Baker, Mary Tudor's chancellor, tortured Protestants before burning them at the stake. Next to the church is Cranbrook School, founded early in the 16th century, although some of the buildings are of later date.

Crawley, *W Sx,* is a large and fast-growing town near the Surrey border on the A21, bypassed by the M23 and extending from Three Bridges in the east to Ifield in the west. The old part of the town has a wide High Street, narrowing at the southern end, with the George Hotel, an old coaching inn where the Prince Regent stopped on his travels to and from Brighton, and the timbered Ancient Prior's restaurant. East of the old town is the vast new shopping complex with its car-parks and pedestrian precincts, and still further east the industrial estate.

Crowborough, *E Sx,* is a town on the A26, 7 miles southwest of Tunbridge Wells. By Sussex standards it is modern, and growing rapidly. Beacon House on Crowborough Beacon, 792 feet above sea level, is the highest inhabited place in Sussex. Conan Doyle lived at Crowborough for a while. So did Richard Jeffries, the naturalist, the house marked by a tablet.

Cuckfield, *W Sx,* pronounced 'Cookfield', still maintains the appearance of a village, although it is now almost a continuation of Haywards Heath, its younger neighbour. The main street, part of the B2036, is hilly, winding and narrow and has difficulty in coping with the heavy and constant traffic. There are some excellent shops and fine buildings, including the 13th-century White Hart Hotel. The parish church stands high, with a splendid view across fields to the distant South Downs. Inside the church there are many monuments to the Burrell family, who lived at 16th-century Ockenden Manor, now a hotel, and a memorial to Charles Sergison of Cuckfield Park, an Elizabethan house with extensive grounds south of the village. There is a Burrell Arms and a Sergison Arms in Haywards Heath.

Darenth, *Kent,* is a small village 2 miles below Dartford, with South Darenth a mile further down the Darent valley. Near the river is the site of a Roman villa, excavated in the 18th century. Bricks from the villa can be seen in the walls of the parish church, which is built on three levels and contains some faded Norman murals.

Dartford, *Kent,* is an ancient town on the old Roman Watling Street near the mouth of the Darent. Little remains of the priory founded by Edward III, but the massive flint-and-stone church, part of which dates from the 11th century, is worth a visit. So are the Spital almshouses. The first English papermill was established here in the 16th century by Sir John Spilman, and there is a monument to him and his wife in the church. Paper is still made in Dartford; there are also chemical and cement works. In the museum, which forms part of the library, are exhibits dating back to prehistoric times. The road leading to the tunnels under the Thames lies east of the town.

Deal, *Kent,* on the east coast, has a long history. It was here that Julius Caesar landed in 55BC after being repulsed at Dover. Perkin Warbeck landed here. It was at Deal that Henry VIII, under the threat of danger from across the Channel, built one of his 'Three Castles that keep the Downs', the Downs being the roadstead within the Goodwin Sands. Anne of Cleves spent her first night in England in the castle. In Nelson's day the harbour was crowded with ships and the streets bustling with mariners; now it is a quieter place, but with much to interest the visitor.

Deal Castle is the main attraction. Completed in 1540 and placed under the control of the Lord Warden of the Cinque Ports, it was small and purely a fortress, with embrasures for guns and the thick walls rounded to deflect shot. The design was new to this country, with six semi-circular bastions projecting from a central keep and an outer curtain, also with six bastions, one of them the gatehouse. The castle changed hands several times during the Civil War but suffered little damage. In the Second World War it received a direct hit from a bomb, but has since been restored. There is a museum in the gatehouse, the exhibits arranged in chronological order.

Deal has two interesting churches, both brick-built – St Leonard's basically Norman, St George's early 18th century. There are two fine golf courses, and north of the town are the ruins Sandown Castle. Sandown was the most northerly of the 'Three Castles that keep the Downs', the most southerly being at Walmer (see below).

Denton, *Kent,* is a tiny village on the A260, 7 miles north of Folkestone, its green surrounded by half-timbered and tiled cottages. To the south are Tappington Hall, a brick-and-timber farmhouse, home of the Barham family (see Snargate), and Denton Court, rebuilt in 1860 after a fire and standing in 200 acres of ground. North of the village is 17th-century Broome Park, once owned by Lord Kitchener and now a hotel.

Devil's Dyke, *E Sx,* (Tour 10), is a large cleft across the southern slope of Dyke Hill, 5 miles north of Brighton. Dyke Hill was an Iron Age fort, and the rampart and ditch that guarded it can be seen in the southwest corner. According to legend, however, the Dyke was not formed by man. The Devil announced that he would drown all the churches of the Weald by letting in the sea between sunset and sunrise and, heedless of the pleadings of St Cuthman, a Sussex saint, he began chopping a way through the Downs. He had nearly completed the task when a Poynings woman, awakened by the noise, lit a candle and looked out of her window to see what was causing it. St Cuthman made the candle glow so brightly that the cocks started to crow, believing it to be sunrise; and the Devil angrily decamped, leaving the Dyke unfinished. Dyke Hill is a favoured take-off point for hang-gliders, who can often be seen swooping over its slopes and the Weald below. It can be reached by a turning off the A2038, on the crest of the Downs.

Ditchling, *E Sx,* (Tour 9) is an attractive village at the foot of the South Downs, its main street hilly and narrow. Opposite the mainly 13th-century church is Wing's Place, a lovely timber-framed Tudor House in 1½ acres of garden. Ditchling has a reputation as a cultural centre, and a small art gallery shows work by local artists; Eric Gill and Frank Brangwyn lived here, and many crafts have been carried on in the village. A mile to the south is Ditchling Beacon, 813 feet up on the Downs with magnificent and extensive views.

Dover, *Kent,* only 21 miles from France and the principal Channel port, has been one of the main gateways to England for centuries. The present harbour, however, is comparatively modern; over a mile long and protected seaward by a break-water. Both the harbour and the town are dominated by Henry II's powerful castle on the East Cliff. Primarily a fortress, it is also a palace and a museum and was continuously garrisoned for nearly 1000 years. The Great Keep, built on three levels with walls up to 22 feet thick, contains many apartments; in and above the forebuilding are two of the finest Norman chapels in existence. Closer to the sea is the Saxon church of St Mary in the Castle, and an artificial mound, probably Saxon in origin, on which stands the Pharos, a 40-ft high Roman lighthouse.

East of Castle Hill is the Bleriot Memorial, marking the spot where the aviator landed his monoplane on 25th July 1909 after the first cross-Channel flight. Nor is Bleriot the only cross-Channeller to be remembered by the town. On Marine Parade there are memorials to Charles Rolls, who in 1910 crossed to France and back in a single flight, and to Captain Webb, the first man to swim the Channel. Behind the parish church of St Mary's in the High Street is the banch where The Barons of the Cinque Ports used to sit; the Lord Warden is also the Constable of Dover Castle. Incorporated in the town hall is the Maison Dieu Hospital, a 13th-century lodging house for pilgrims; near-by are the town museum and St Edmund's Chapel, the latter believed to be the smallest church in regular use in England.

Near the roundabout at the start of the Folkestone Road is Dover College, a boys' public school built among the ruins of a 12th-century priory. On the Western Heights is the Citadel, built during the Napoleonic Wars and now a gaol. Still further west is the sheer drop of Shakespeare Cliff, the 'chalky bourn' where Edgar, disguised as a peasant, brought the blinded Gloucester in *King Lear.*

Dungeness, *Kent,* is a large expanse of barren shingle thrusting out into the Channel, the shingle constantly shifting. It is a windswept place, a favourite with sea anglers. There has been a light of sorts on the point for nearly 300 years, but the first lighthouse was built at the end of the 18th century; left stranded inland as the sea receded, it was turned into homes for the keepers and replaced by the present automatic lighthouse. The most striking building on Dungeness is the atomic power station, which started generating electricity in 1965 and can be visited by arrangement. There are gravel pits, the lifeboat station, a few fishermen's cottages and the bird sanctuary at Boulderwall. Dungeness is also the southern terminus of the Romney, Hythe and Dymchurch railway. (See below.)

Dymchurch, *Kent,* (Tour 5) is the 'capital' of Romney Marsh and a popular seaside resort. Despite the inevitable amusement arcades and gift shops, the car-parks and caravans, the village itself is charming. The New Hall, 'new' in 1580 when it replaced one destroyed by fire, was the old meeting house of the Lords of Romney Marsh and now contains a small museum. Down by the front is Dymchurch Wall, a Roman barrier against the sea which has twice been reconstructed, and a Martello Tower containing exhibits connected with the Napoleonic Wars. To readers of detective fiction Dymchurch is perhaps best known as the scene of the exploits of Dr Syn, Russell Thorndike's fictional vicar.

Eastbourne, *E Sx.* An elegant town and holiday resort with a population of 72 000, its seafront is landscaped and free of shops, with a fine pier and some handsome hotels and well-kept gardens. What Bexhill owes to the de la Warr family, Eastbourne owes to the Devonshires. It was William Cavendish, the 7th Duke, who started the development of the old village of East Bourne in the mid 19th century, and the family's association with the town is marked by statues and place names.

The main part of the seafront stretches for over a mile, from the Royal Parade to King Edward's Parade. At the northern end is the Redoubt Tower, brick built and solid, with the Aquarium and a model village. At the southern end is the Wish Tower ('wish' derives from the Saxon *wisc*, meaning a marshy place), now a museum, with the Lifeboat Museum beside it and Devonshire Park and the Winter Garden across the parade. Two miles further south is Beachy Head, reached by a steeply winding road. Beachy Head is spectacular: a green sward ending abruptly in a chalk precipice over 500 feet high, dwarfing the lighthouse at its base.

In addition to its obvious seaside attractions, Eastbourne has much to offer the visitor. There are two theatres and a fine library. For sportsmen there are internationally famous tennis courts and bowling greens, a 'royal' golf course and a county cricket ground. In the old town, at the northern tip of Gildredge Park, is the Towner Art Gallery, formerly the old Manor House. Across Church Road from the Art Gallery is St Mary's, the 12th-century parish church, and nearby is the Lambe Hotel, which claims to date from the 13th century.

Eastchurch, *Kent,* is an attractive village on the Isle of Sheppey and the site of the first British airfield, where both Lord Brabazon of Tara and Sir Winston Churchill learned to fly. Nearby are the ruins of Shurland Hall, where Henry VIII and Anne Boleyn spent their honeymoon. Shurland Hall was built by Sir Thomas Cheyney from stone brought from Chilham Castle. (See above.)

East Grinstead, *W Sx,* (Tour 7). The High Street of this market town, with its many attractive half-timbered houses, has been relieved of its former congestion by a new bypass. At the top of the town is Sackville College, an almshouse set in a pleasant quadrangle and founded by the Earl of Dorset in 1609; the Rev John Mason Neale, author of many well-known hymns, was warden of the college in the mid 19th century. The church is nearby, screened from the bustle of the High Street. Outside the porch are grave slabs in memory of three Protestant martyrs who were burned at the stake in the High Street in 1556.

Like nearby Withyham and Hartfield, East Grinstead has its Dorset Arms, here an old Georgian inn opposite the church. North of the High Street, along the A264, is the Queen Victoria Hospital, made famous by the plastic surgery carried out by Sir Archibald McIndoe during and after the Second World War. It was here that the Guinea Pig Club was formed for aircrew who had suffered severe burns or facial injuries. Down a turning off the B2110 to the south is Standen (see below).

East Malling, *Kent,* (Tour 3). There are a number of old buildings around the church, but the population has grown to such an extent that it now exceeds that of West Malling, with new estates, complete with schools, at Clare Park. East Malling is chiefly notable for its Research Station, familiar to fruit growers all over the world. The headquarters of the station are at Bradbourne (NT), an 18th-century manor house which was once the home of Sir Roger Twisden, the High Court judge who sent John Bunyan to prison.

Ebbsfleet, *Kent,* on the shore of Pegwell Bay, is a historic spot. It was here that the Jutes under Hengist and Horsa landed in 449, an event commemorated 1500 years later by a Danish crew, who sailed a replica of the original dragon-ship across the Channel in 1949. Their ship, the Hugin, is displayed in a field. 150 years after the Jutes St Augustine also landed at Ebbsfleet to begin his conversion of pagan Britain. A Celtic cross marks the spot where, at the invitation of King Ethelred, he preached his first sermon.

Edenbridge, *Kent,* along the B2026, 5 miles south of Westerham, is a village that has straggled into a town. There is industry here including a 300-year old tannery; but the town centre has retained much of its medieval charm, with some fine old houses, including the Crown Inn and the Priest House near the church.

Elham, *Kent,* (Tour 2), is one of the loveliest villages in the county. There are some beautiful timbered and tile-hung houses, including the 15th-century Abbot's Fireside restaurant and the old manor house, which once belonged to the Wotton family. The impressive 13th-century church, its tower topped by a gleaming lead spire, is decorated inside and out with some magnificent carving and panelling.

Eynsford, *Kent,* (Tour 6), is situated in the Darent valley. The village centre is away from the heavy traffic on the main road and provides an attractive scene with trim half-timbered houses, a Norman church and an old bridge over the river. Much of the curtain wall of the castle, built around 1100, still stands. A mile south of Eynsford are Lullingstone Castle and Roman Villa (see below).

Fairlight, *E Sx,* is a tiny village 4 miles east of Hastings, with Fairlight Cove its outlet to the sea. The area is now a National Park, with 58 acres of cliff-land, and this has saved it from the string of chalets and car-parks that has spoiled so much of the coastline elsewhere. The cliffs are over 500 feet high, and from the tall tower of the parish church there are magnificent views inland to Romney Marsh and the Weald and seaward across the Channel to France.

Farningham, *Kent,* the centre of a market-gardening area, is situated 5 miles south of Dartford at the junction of the A20 and A225, with the M20 to the north. Despite its proximity to main roads the old village is delightful, with a wide main street and an 18th-century bridge over the river Darent. The 13th-century church has a battlemented tower, and a unique 15th-century font carved with representations of the Sacraments. Captain Bligh (of the *Bounty*) once lived in the manor house, in the grounds of which is a 1st-century Roman villa. The 18th-century Lion Hotel has a 17th-century cottage at the rear.

Faversham, *Kent,* is an ancient borough situated north of the A2 between Sittingbourne and Canterbury, at the head of Faversham Creek. It is an attractive town, with wide streets and some fine Tudor and Georgian buildings; the guildhall and the 16th-century grammar school, now a masonic hall, are arcaded, supported by the original pillars. The interior of the parish church presents an interesting contrast of styles and periods and the steeple, visible from all directions, is unusual in its design. Faversham was an important port in the Middle Ages and still enjoys a certain amount of coastal trade, but brewing is now the main industry. Foundations of King Stephen's great 12th-century abbey, 300 feet long, were discovered in 1965, but all that remains standing is the old guest house, known as Arden's House. Arden, a 16th-century mayor of Faversham, was murdered here by two men hired by his wife and her lover. The culprits were hanged, executed or burnt at the stake, and their story was later turned into the lurid Elizabethan melodrama, *Arden of Faversham.*

***Fishbourne Roman Palace,** *W Sx,* (Tour 12), is one of the most important archaeological discoveries of this century, for there is nothing remotely like it elsewhere in Britain. Built around 75AD and destroyed some 200 years later, the palace is laid out under an enormous hangar, with walk-ways round the mosaic-covered floors and a fascinating museum. The gardens contain plants the Romans are known to have used, and the whole area covers over 10 acres.

Fittleworth, *W Sx,* (Tour 11). The church stands on high ground at the northern end of the village, with a 12th-century tower and candlesticks on the pews. Fittleworth is unusual in having three bridges at its southern end; opposite one is a watermill, the wheel in ruins but the mill itself in a good state of repair. Another bridge crosses the Rother and the third is over what was once the railway line but is now a pleasant walk. In Fittleworth Woods is Brinkwells, an 18th-century house where Elgar lived for a time and wrote several of his major works.

Fletching, *E Sx,* (Tour 9). It was in Fletching church, an early 13th-century building with a Norman tower, that Simon de Montfort spent the night in prayer before the Battle of Lewes. Edward Gibbon is buried in the mausoleum.

Folkestone, *Kent,* is a charming and dignified seaside resort, somewhat Victorian in character, which evolved from a fishing village with the coming of the railway in the mid 19th century. Hotels line the front, and between them and the sea are the Leas, a cliff-top expanse of lawns and flowers and shrubs and walks that stretch down to the promenade below. The pedestrian-only High Street is steep and narrow, with the parish church of St Mary and St Eanswythe at the top of the hill. Eanswythe, grand-daughter of King Ethelbert and the patron saint of Folkestone, founded a nunnery here in 630 which was later sacked by Danish raiders and never restored; in the 19th century her bones were discovered in the sanctuary wall and are kept in a shrine.

A mile inland from the town is Caesar's Camp, a chalk hill which was probably the site of an Iron Age fortification, with the mysterious Sugarloaf Hill to the east. But Folkestone is not concerned wholly with the past. It is a cross-Channel port, the harbour protected by the East Pier. Below the Leas and the Marine Parade are bathing and boating pools, the Pavilion and an amusement park. There is an Arts Centre at the New Metropole. The Sports Centre above Radnor Park has extensive facilities, including an artificial ski slope.

Fordwich, *Kent,* (Tour 1) is situated on the River Stour. In the Middle Ages it was the port for Canterbury, where Caen stone for the cathedral and wine for the monks were unloaded. It is a borough, with its own mayor, and a timbered town hall that is the smallest in Kent. Inside the church is a stone sarcophagus, traditionally the burial chest of St Augustine but more likely Norman work, and a wooden chair cut from a solid piece of oak.

Forest Row, *E Sx,* is largely residential and lies at the junction of the A22 and B2110, 3 miles south of East Grinstead. The town hall in the centre of the village was built at the end of the 19th century by the Freshfield family, who lived at nearby Kidbrooke Park. The ruins of 17th-century Brambletye House can be seen from the main road as it climbs the hill to East Grinstead.

*Springhill Wildfowl Park is down a turning off the Turner's Hill road. Here there are over 1000 waterfowl of 100 species   49

from all over the world wandering freely around an enclosed 10 acres. There is a picnic area and car-park, from which there is a magnificent view across the Weir Wood reservoir, dotted with small sailing boats, to East Grinstead church towering over the town on the opposite hill.

Gads Hill, *Kent,* on the A226 west of Rochester, has associations with both Shakespeare and Dickens. It was at Gadshill that, in *Henry IV,* Sir John Falstaff, in company with his band of thieves, robbed and bound travellers en route for Canterbury, only to have their spoils taken from them by Prince Hal and Poins. On the site of this fictitious encounter is the Sir John Falstaff Inn, and almost opposite is Gads Hill Place, where Dickens spent the last 15 years of his life. He had coveted the house since his youth and bought it in 1856. He was working on *Edwin Drood,* in a chalet in the garden, when he died.

Glynde, *E Sx,* (Tour 9) is a quiet, picturesque village 3 miles east of Lewes. The 18th-century parish church is flint-built, the interior draped with hessian. To the west is Mount Caburn, a prominent landmark that was once a Celtic settlement. North of the village is Glyndebourne, the internationally famous opera house founded by John Christie, who inherited the estate and staged his first opera in 1934. Many of the world's finest artistes have performed here; the grounds are delightful, with clipped yew hedges and lawns sweeping down to a tree-lined stream. Opposite the church is *Glynde Place, a magnificent flint-built Elizabethan mansion which was originally the home of the Morley family. In the 18th century it passed by marriage to the Trevors, who reconstructed much of the interior and whose portraits dominate the Long Gallery. Wooden columns in the Georgian hall have been painted to resemble marble.

***Godinton Park,** *Kent,* (Tour 4). The house is separated from the park by enormous topiary yew hedges. The present building is mainly early 17th century, the work of Captain Nicholas Toke, although the original house was considerably older. The Great Hall is distinguished by magnificent wood panelling and carving; so is the Great Chamber upstairs, with a frieze of wooden soldiers carved below the ceiling. There is magnificent carving too on the staircase, and the Priest's Room has a carved confessional box. Apart from remodelling the house, Captain Toke's passion was for all forms of hunting; but his energetic way of life in no way diminished his health or virility. He was 93 when he died, hurrying to London to look for a sixth wife.

Goodwood, *W Sx,* (Tour 12) is a vast estate with Goodwood House, ancestral home of the Dukes of Richmond and Gordon, at its centre. Goodwood Park stretches up the hill to the racecourse where Trundle Hill, an Iron Age fortified settlement, now serves as a grandstand; there is also a golf course, an airfield and a motor circuit, the latter now used only for testing.
Goodwood House is based on an old Jacobean house, bought by the first Duke. The present structure dates mainly from the end of the 18th century, designed by the architect James Wyatt for the 3rd Duke; large as it is, it would have been larger still had not the money run out. The house contains beautiful pieces of 18th-century furniture, Sèvres porcelain and Gobelin tapestries, and there are paintings by Vandyke, Canaletto, Stubbs and other famous artists, including a Lely portrait of Frances Stuart holding Minerva's spear and used as a model for Britannia on British coins.

Goudhurst, *Kent,* (Tour 4). The main street slopes up a hill-side, its houses an intriguing mixture of styles, with the pond at the bottom and the manor house, the old inn and the church at the top. Inside the church, which is largely 15th century, are marvellously detailed memorials to the Culpepers, a family famous in Kent; from the tower, which stands 500 feet above sea level and is generally open to the public, there is a splendid view of the village and the orchards and hop-gardens beyond. In the 18th century, when smuggling was rife in Kent, the area around Goudhurst was terrorized by a gang of smugglers from Hawkhurst, led by the Kingsmill brothers. Eventually the men of the village were formed into a militia to deal with them, and in the ensuing shoot-out one of the Kingsmills was killed. A year later the other was hanged.

Gravesend, *Kent,* a town with a population of some 54 000, is situated on the Thames estuary. Historically important – in the past whole fleets used to anchor here – modern building has spoilt its character; but there is still considerable riverside activity and it is the station for the Thames pilots. The parish church was rebuilt in the 18th century after a fire which destroyed much of the old town. The Indian princess Pocahontas died in Gravesend in 1617 on her way back to Virginia and was buried under the chancel of the old church. There is a statue to her memory in the churchyard.

*****Great Comp,** *Kent,* (Tour 6) near Borough Green is a 17th-century house whose owners, Mr and Mrs Cameron, have over the past 23 years constructed around it a beautiful garden of lawns and paths covering 7 acres, with a fine collection of trees, shrubs, heathers and herbaceous plants. A Music Festival is held in September in the old stable, now converted into a concert hall, when parts of the garden are floodlit.

Groombridge, (Tour 7), is partly in Kent and partly in East Sussex. At the foot of a steep winding hill, the triangular green is flanked north and west by a pleasant inn and some tile-hung cottages. To the east is Groombridge Place and the church. Groombridge Place, not open to the public but visible from the footpath along the lake, is a splendid Jacobean manor house across a moat. The church at its gates dates from the same period.

Hailsham, *E Sx,* 8 miles north of Eastbourne, is one of the oldest market towns in the country, having been granted its charter in 1252. The manor house is early 18th century, and there are some good Georgian buildings in the High Street. The church is 15th century, with a pinnacled tower. Rope has been made in Hailsham for centuries.

Harbledown, *Kent,* is a village on the A2, just outside Canterbury, and the last stopping place of the pilgrims on their way to Becket's shrine; from the hill they would have had their first view of the cathedral. Lanfranc founded a leper hospital here in 1086, from which Henry II walked barefoot to the cathedral as a penance for Becket's murder. The hospital chapel remains, but the rest of the present building is Victorian and in use as almshouses. Visitors are welcome.

Hardham, *W Sx,* is a small village south of Pulborough on the A29, its principal attraction being the many wall paintings in St Botolph's. They date back over 800 years, and there is little in the country to match them. Scenes depicting the life of St George are the earliest known paintings of the saint in England; others show Adam and Eve in the Garden of Eden. The church is probably Saxon in origin, but the village existed in Roman times and was the first posting station on Stane Street (see below). South of the church are the remains of an Augustinian Priory, the walls incorporated in a farmhouse.

Hastings, *E Sx,* a coastal holiday resort and fishing town, is famous in history as the scene of the Battle of Hastings, which actually took place further north, at Battle (see above). The old part of the town is at the eastern end, in a valley between West

Hill and East Hill, with steep alleys leading down to well-preserved streets and attractive houses; to the antique shops and the old town hall, now a museum; and to the medieval churches of All Saints, where Titus Oates was once the curate, and St Clements. Both churches suffered severe damage during French raids in the 14th century and have largely been rebuilt. The Catholic church of St Mary Star of the Sea, with its pebbled walls, is also here; it was founded by the poet Coventry Patmore, the stables of whose old house are now a theatre. In the bowels of West Hill are St Clement's caves, natural underground passages elaborated for commercial use and used as air-raid shelters during the Second World War. Further along the ridge is William of Normandy's castle, hastily erected and now a ruin, with a fine view of the shoreline and across the town to St Leonards. Below Castle Hill is George Street, the wares in its shops and cafés redolent of the sea, and the Fishermen's Museum. The latter was originally a chapel and houses the *Enterprise*, last of the sailing luggers.

Hastings and St Leonards (see below) have merged into one, with a population of some 75 000 and a 2-mile stretch of shingle beach. Opposite Hastings pier are White Rock Gardens, with a Model Village and a Pavilion faintly reminiscent of Brighton's Royal Pavilion. The White Rock Pavilion is one of the town's main attractions, for in addition to a fine concert hall it houses the Hastings Historical Embroidery, 243 feet long and 3 feet high, depicting 81 episodes in British history from 1066 to the present day. The embroidery was made in 1966 to mark the 900th anniversary of the Battle of Hastings and is on view in the summer.

Haywards Heath, *W Sx,* is a straggling town on the A272, with a population of 26 000; on the London to Brighton railway line, it provides a quick and constant train service to both towns and is therefore much favoured by commuters. With Burgess Hill it forms the main shopping centre between Crawley and Brighton, and has reasonable facilities for sports and the arts.

Headcorn, *Kent,* (Tour 4). Although largely a commuter village it retains much of its Wealden charm. It was once a cloth town, and the old Cloth Hall is an attractive building. So is Shakespeare House, though it has no direct connection with the playwright. Behind the church, with its massive tower, is Headcorn Manor, built early in the 16th century for the parson.

Heathfield, *E Sx,* 7 miles east of Uckfield on the A265, covers a wide area and has more or less absorbed the surrounding hamlets. On a ridge east of the village is the Blackdown Windmill, brought by horse and cart from Sissinghurst in the mid 19th century to replace one that had been burnt down. Beyond the wall that marks the boundary of Heathfield Park is the Gibraltar Tower, a castellated folly erected in honour of General Sir George Elliot's defence of the Rock between 1779 and 1783.

Hellingly, *E Sx,* is a small, compact village 2 miles north of Hailsham, with one of the largest mental hospitals in the country. The Norman church stands in the middle of an ancient barrow, with the houses clustered round it; an interesting feature is the chancel, set askew to the nave. Near the church is the quaintly named 15th-century Horselunges Manor, one of the finest timber-framed houses in the county.

Herne Bay, *Kent.* A quiet 19th-century seaside town 8½ miles north of Canterbury, it was popular with the Victorians. There is an ornate clock tower on the front and a pier nearly a mile long, second only to that of Southend; the pier pavilion was burnt down in 1969. South of the town is the attractive village of Herne, with a 200-year old smock mill.

****Hever Castle,** *Kent,* (Tour 7), is a 13th-century manor house surrounded by a moat, complete with battlemented keep, drawbridge and gatehouse, the outer of the two original portcullises remaining being the only genuine wooden portcullis still in working order in England. Built by Walter de Hevere in 1462, the castle was bought by Sir Geoffrey Bullen and inherited in 1505 by his grandson Thomas, later to become the Earl of Ormonde and Wiltshire. In 1533 Sir Thomas's daughter Anne, who had changed 'Bullen' to 'Boleyn', married Henry VIII; three years later she was executed, and on her father's death Henry gave the castle to his divorced wife Anne of Cleves. For the next 350 years it was owned successively by the Waldegraves, the Humphreys and the Waldos until, in 1903, it was bought by William Waldorf Astor, who built a Tudor village to house his guests and his servants and created a beautiful garden and park around the artificial lake.

The castle contains some fine wood panelling and plasterwork, particularly in the Long Gallery. Among the many and varied contents are pictures by Holbein, Titian, Clouet and other famous artists, 15th and 16th century Burgundian and Flemish tapestries, magnificent suits of armour in the dining and entrance halls and, in the keep, a collection of medieval instruments of torture.

54

Hever Castle

Highdown Hill, *W Sx,* (NT), 3 miles northwest of Worthing, is a unique site of great archaeological importance: a Late Bronze Age settlement underlying an Early Iron-Age hill-fort, which was itself reoccupied in the 3rd century AD. Earlier excavation had discovered a pagan Saxon cemetery within the ramparts of the fort.

Highdown Hill is also the burial place of John Olliver, known as the 'Mad Miller' or the 'Melancholy Miller', who worked the mill which, until 1826, stood on top of the hill with his cottage nearby. A cheerful and religious man, he was fascinated by death, and in 1766, at the age of 57, he bought a site on the hill and built himself a mausoleum of brick and stone; being something of a poet, he inscribed it with suitable verses and surrounded it with iron railings. His coffin was also ready, kept under his bed. When eventually he died, in 1793, his funeral was fittingly bizarre. Thousands came to see the wheeled coffin trundled round a field, attended by girls dressed in white with one of the girls reading a sermon. The mausoleum became a favourite picnic place, with Olliver's widow serving teas from the little summerhouse where her late husband had been wont to sit and contemplate his future resting place. The mausoleum is still there, tucked away behind Highdown Chalk Garden.

The garden is unique, created over 50 years by the late Sir Frederick Stern and his wife, with an astonishing variety of wonderful flowers, shrubs and trees. Open all the year round (although not at week-ends in winter), the garden is at its best in the spring.

Horsham, *W Sx,* is 8 miles southwest from Crawley along the A264, with a population of 27 000. The town centre has recently been redeveloped, linking the old narrow streets with underpasses and shopping precincts. Behind the old town hall is the Causeway, a cul-de-sac of ancient houses; Causeway House, which dates from the 16th century, is now a museum specializing in local material. At the end of the Causeway is the church, with a 12th-century tower and a simple memorial to Percy Bysshe Shelley. Shelley was born in nearby Warnham (see below), and lived for a while at Highley Manor, near Balcombe (see above).

Horsted Keynes, *W Sx,* is an attractive village on the fringe of Ashdown Forest, 4½ miles northeast of Haywards Heath; the 'Keynes', pronounced 'Kanes', derives from 'de Cahainges', a Norman knight who came over with William the Conqueror. The main street runs through a well-kept green, with an inn on either side. The Crown Inn, popular locally for its food, is guarded by a magnificent monkey-puzzle tree and is a scheduled building; originally a farmhouse, it was first licensed to sell liquour in 1734. New estates are out of sight of the main part of the village. The Norman church, with its curious pygmy-size effigy of a crusader, is tucked away at the end of a lane; beside it a wide track leads through woodland and past lakes to Broadlands, a lovely 15th-century manor house which is now a home for drug addicts.

Hove, *E Sx,* is so close to Brighton that the two are often classed as one, but it is a large and elegant town with a population of 90 000. As in Brighton, the front has its big hotels and large blocks of flats, with well-tended lawns between them and the sea; along the esplanade is a cheerful row of brightly painted bathing chalets. Tall, stylish houses line the squares and the wide avenues that sweep up from the front, with the Grand Avenue the most impressive. Impressive too are Brunswick Square and Palmeira Square, the latter the funnel through which Palmeira Avenue leads to the shops and the County cricket ground. The wide main shopping street has a dignified air, typical of Hove as a whole. Among the town's many attractions are the Engineerium, the Floral Clock, and the Brocke Scented Garden for the Blind.

Howletts Zoo Park, *Kent,* is at Bekesbourne, 3 miles southeast of Canterbury, and is the creation of John Aspinall, who also owns Port Lympne (see below). Here are gathered over 40 different species of wild animals, from every continent, in a 15th-century park which contains some magnificent trees, including a giant sequoia in the Woodland Walk and a turkey oak with a spread of 140 feet.

Cape Buffalo, Howletts Zoo Park

Hurstpierpoint, *W Sx,* (Tour 10), is a small town with a twisting High Street lined by mainly Georgian houses. The tall 19th-century church contains medieval effigies of the de Pierpoint family, whose ancestral home was at Danny, below Wolstonbury Hill. Danny, an Elizabethan manor considerably altered at the beginning of the 18th century, was leased to Lloyd George at the end of the First World War, and it was here that the terms for the Armistice were drawn up. The house is now split into flats. North of the town is Hurstpierpoint College, one of the Woodward public schools.

Hythe, *Kent,* (Tour 2), one of the Cinque Ports, now stands inland, its harbour lost in shingle. Built on terraces many of the streets and alleys are steep and narrow, but from the higher levels there is an excellent view out to sea. The medieval church of St Leonard's, situated at one of the highest points, is one of the finest in Kent, cathedral-like in proportions. The canal, once a defensive waterway, has attractive gardens lining its banks and is used for boating and the staging of water carnivals. North of the town is Sandling Park, with its beautiful woodland walks, a blaze of colour in summer.

Ide Hill, *Kent,* (Tour 6). This tiny village is high on a wooded ridge (NT) overlooking the Weald. The view is one of the most magnificent to be found anywhere, enhanced by the vast area of Bough Beech reservoir, a Mecca for fishermen and small boat sailors. The clock on the church tower is reputed to be the highest in the county.

**Emmetts,* ½ mile north of the village is also owned by the National Trust. The house is closed to the public, but the 4 acre   57 garden may be visited. It is one of the highest gardens in Kent, with some rare trees and shrubs, best seen in spring and autumn.

*__Ightham Mote__, *Kent,* (Tour 6), near the village of Ivy Hatch, is one of the best known moated houses in the country. It is a greystone manor with an imposing gatehouse, brought to its perfection by the Cawne and Selby families, whose tombs and memorials can be seen in Ightham church. There are huge oak beams in the Great Hall and a carved Jacobean oak frieze in the drawing room. The house has two chapels, one medieval and one Tudor, the latter with a sanctuary ring for the protection of criminals. On the northern side a small watergate leads to the moat.

__Itchenor,__ *W Sx,* lies on the west coast of the Selsey Peninsula, the approach road lined by well-kept modern houses set in woodland. The harbour presents a delightful prospect of yachts, fishing boats and small cruisers, and there is a pleasant walk in either direction along the waterfront. Emmets, a small hotel noted for the imaginative excellence of its cuisine, is a 17th-century building with an attractive garden; the name derives from the initial letters of the Christian names of the children who once lived there.

__Itchingfield,__ *W Sx.* A tiny village 3 miles southwest of Horsham, south of the A264, its main attraction is the belfry tower of the Norman church; 600 years old, the oak beams are fastened together by oak pegs. A mile to the south is Christ's Hospital, founded by Edward VI in 1553, which was moved from London in 1902. The dining hall and speech hall are vast, as are the murals on their walls and the chapel and quadrangle. Visitors are welcome, and there are occasional guided tours in the summer.

__Kenardington,__ *Kent,* (Tour 5). The 13th-century church, tucked away down a side lane, has an outside stair turret; nearby are remains of earthworks thought to have been built by King Alfred as protection against the Danes. Kenardington Manor, dating from around 1500, stands on the site of an earlier Norman house.

__Kits Coty,__ *Kent,* (Tour 3) are prehistoric remains reached by a path from the foot of Bluebell Hill. They are the most spectacular of the megalithic monuments in the county, consisting of four huge stones, three upright and one horizontal, on the hillside overlooking the Medway. Lower down is Little Kits Coty, a collection of half-buried stones.

Kentish Farm, Lamberhurst

Lamberhurst, *Kent,* (Tour 4), was once partly in Sussex. It is a long village, with some typical Kentish houses and inns. Once engaged in the iron industry – the railings for St Paul's Cathedral were cast here – it turned to hop growing when the industry declined. To increase intimacy with a dwindling congregation the church altar has been moved to the north wall and the pews turned to face it.

*Scotney Castle (NT), a Gothic stone house built by Edward Hussey in 1837, lies just south of the village. Down the hill are the ruins of the old castle, a Tudor mansion in brick added to a small fortified manor house. Now little remains apart from the moat and the 14th-century tower, but it is Edward Hussey's garden that attracts the visitors. An old quarry was turned into an alpine garden, and in early summer there is a magnificent display of rhododendrons and azaleas.

Lancing, *W Sx,* consisting of North Lancing and South Lancing, is situated between Shoreham and Worthing. South Lancing is a seaside resort with a good beach. North Lancing lies a mile inland and has a typical Norman Church. Lancing College, one of the Woodward public schools for boys, is northeast of the town. The college chapel is enormous, with cathedral-like proportions, the nave being over 90 feet high. It was built over many years by local craftsmen using local materials, the foundation stone having been laid in 1868. The colourful tapestries behind the altar are three of the largest in the world.

***Leeds Castle,** *Kent,* (Tour 3), is one of the loveliest in Europe. Both buildings and setting are magnificent. The castle stands   59

on two islands in a lagoon formed from the River Len, the islands connected by a stone bridge. There has been a castle at Leeds since Norman times, and Edward I's gatehouse and the walls of the old barbican still stand. After 300 years as a royal castle it was respectively owned by the St Legers, the Culpepers and the Fairfaxes; and finally by Lady Baillie, who devoted nearly 50 years of her life to its restoration and improvement, and bequeathed it to the nation. The castle is full of magnificent tapestries, carpets and furniture – the table top in Henry VIII's Banqueting Hall is made from a single plank – and there are paintings by Tiepolo, Pissarro, Degas and other famous artists. The park is a delightful place in which to stroll or picnic, with some fine trees and many rare birds around the lakes and gardens.

Lenham, *Kent,* 8 miles southeast of Maidstone, is a typically medieval village, with the square enclosed by old timbered buildings, among them the Dog and Bear Inn where Queen Anne once stayed. In the church is the tombstone of Mary Honeywood, who left 367 descendants when she died at the age of 92. A war memorial in the form of a cross, cut into neighbouring fields, forms a prominent landmark.

*****Leonardslee Gardens,** *W Sx,* (Tour 10). From the lawns of a Victorian house, paths lead through huge banks of rhododendrons to a valley, along the sides of which the gardens extend, the colours of the flowers reflected in the pools below. Leonardslee was begun in 1887 by Sir Edmund Loder, after whom the *Loderi* rhododendrons are named.

Lewes, *E Sx,* (Tour 9), the old county town, stands on a hill on the A27, the congestion in its narrow winding streets being relieved to some extent by a bypass. Dominating the High Street and the town is the castle, built by William de Warenne, the Conqueror's son-in-law, and unique in having two mottes. Never besieged, many of the buildings were demolished in 1620 and used as building material; but much of the original walls remain, although the barbican is early 14th century.

Near the castle entrance is Barbican House, a museum containing a collection of ancient coins and some beautiful Saxon jewellery. Also in the High Street are the 15th-century Bull House, once the home of Tom Paine, author of *The Rights of Man,* and two fine Georgian hotels: the White Hart, an old coaching inn, and Shelley's, which once belonged to the poet's family. Narrow little alleys, or 'twittens', run steeply down to Southover High Street and Anne of Cleves House.
Anne of Cleves House, is a 15th-century timber-framed house, given to the 'Flanders Mare' by Henry VIII on their divorce. It is now a folk museum, with a fine collection of ancient ironwork. In the kitchen is a black marble table top from Malling House where, according to legend, the murderers of Thomas à Becket rested after riding from Canterbury. When they threw their arms on the table it collapsed – in revulsion, presumably, at the crime they had committed!

In the mid 13th century Lewes boasted ten churches, and the oldest still standing is St Anne's, a fine Norman building with a Jacobean pulpit, outside the West Gate. Below the castle is St Michael's, with its round tower and twisting spire, and down in the valley is the parish church of St John's, built by William de Warenne after the Battle of Hastings. In the fields beyond the church are the ruins of the great Cluniac Priory of St Pancras, destroyed at the Dissolution in 1537, and where Henry III had his headquarters before the Battle of Lewes in 1264. It was in the grounds of the priory that workmen engaged in the construction of the Lewes-Brighton railway in 1845 unearthed two lead coffins containing the bodies of William de Warenne and his wife Gundrada, which now rest in a side chapel of St John's. The workmen also unearthed a more grisly find: an enormous quantity of human bones, the remains of men killed in the Battle of Lewes (1500 skeletons had previously been dug up in the vicinity of Lewes Gaol, where the heaviest fighting is believed to have occurred) and presumably buried by the monks. Ten railway carriages were needed to cart the bones away – to be used as rubble in the construction of an embankment! (See also Offham).

Lindfield, *W Sx,* (Tour 10), now practically an eastern extension of Haywards Heath, has yet managed to retain its individuality. The main street is one of the most picturesque in Sussex. At the foot of the hill is the village pond, with a fascinating semi-circle of small houses around the far side, and beyond the pond the large green. All the buildings that line the main street have beauty of one kind or another, but it is those at the top end that attract the most attention. Here are gathered a cluster of fine Queen Anne and Georgian houses, with Old Place, a gabled and timber-framed Tudor house opposite the large 13th-century church, taking pride of place. The thatched cottage next door is reputed to have been Henry VIII's hunting lodge. Charles Dickens often visited Froyles, an Elizabethan house in the main street. Out on the Ardingly road is Paxhill, a fine Elizabethan manor set high on a hill, built in 1595 and now a nursing home.

Littlehampton, *W Sx,* is a seaside resort 8½ miles from Worthing, with a wide beach and sandy dunes that compensate for the lack of a pier or a promenade. Like Shoreham, it was a busy port in medieval times, but its importance waned with the decline in imports of Caen stone, used in the construction of so many old Sussex churches. The buildings, including the parish church, are mainly Victorian or later. The museum specializes in local exhibits, including Roman pottery and jewellery.

Luddesdown, *Kent,* is a small village 5 miles southeast of Gravesend. Remote against the Downs, Luddesdown Court, the manor house is said to be the oldest house in the country to be continuously occupied, with Bishop Odo probably its first occupant. L-shaped, with flint walls nearly three feet thick, the main rooms are on the first floor, reached by an outside staircase. The medieval stone fireplace in the Great Hall is intact, and there are patches of medieval plasterwork on the walls. Luddesdown Court can be visited by arrangement.

*****Lullingstone Castle,** *Kent,* (Tour 6), in the Darent valley, is an imposing three-storied Tudor mansion, of Norman origin, surrounded by lakes and rich parkland. In 1522 it came into the possession of Sir Percyvall Hart, and by marriage in the 18th century to the Hart Dykes, who have owned it since. The interior has changed little since Tudor times. Queen Anne was a frequent visitor, and the staircase leading to her apartment has shallow treads to accommodate her considerable bulk. The adjacent flint church of St Botolph is full of tombs and monuments of previous occupants of the castle.

***Lullingstone Roman Villa,** *Kent,* (Tour 6), built originally in the 1st century, was later enlarged into a luxury residence, with a bathing suite equipped with under-floor heating and a new kitchen block and servants quarters. The picture mosaics on the floors of the dining and reception rooms are magnificently preserved, and the villa is unique in being the only example in Roman Britain containing a chapel within its wall. Open daily.

Lydd, *Kent,* (Tour 5). Exposed to winds off the sea, it is a cold place and is no longer a port, being situated more than 2 miles inland. In the area are an army camp, an airport and a nuclear power station, but the town still has character. The church shows traces of both Saxon and Norman predecessors; it was severely damaged in the war, but has been tastefully repaired, incorporating some beautiful modern glass and a high vaulted tower.

Lyminge, *Kent,* (Tour 2), has suffered from modern development. But it has a long history, and traces of Saxon, Roman and Norman handiwork can be seen in the church. Lyminge was the centre of Christianity in England during St Ethelburga's lifetime, and she was buried here in 647. Sibton Hall, built in the reign of Queen Anne, is now a girls' school.

Lympne, *Kent,* (Tour 5). Here are Lympne Castle and Port Lympne Zoo Park and Gardens (see below). Down the hill are the remains of a Roman fort, many of the stones from which were used to build the castle. North of the village is Ashford airport, the oldest service airfield in the country, from where Amy Johnson took off on her historic flight to Cape Town in 1932.
**Lympne Castle,* the 14th-century fortified manor house, stands on a hill next to the medieval church, with superb views across Romney Marsh. Restored early this century, it replaced a previous house on the site, built by Lanfranc for the Archbishops of Canterbury. The main feature of the castle is its magnificent hall.
Port Lympne comprises an early 20th-century house and gardens and a magnificent Zoo Park. The house, built by Sir Herbert Baker for Sir Philip Sassoon, is in the Dutch Colonial style, with a Moorish courtyard and an octagonal library specially built for the signing of the Treaty of Paris in 1921. The 15-acre garden, with its great stairway of York stone leading down to the western terrace, contains many beautiful trees and plants and provides a magnificent view over the Channel. But the Zoo Park is Port Lympne's main attraction: 300 acres of

parkland through which a two-mile trek enables the visitor to admire some 30 species of wild animals roaming their carefully designed enclosures.

Port Lympne House

Maidstone, *Kent,* split by the Medway, is the county town with a population of 72 000. Although it has the appearance of modernity, stone implements found in the area indicate that it was once a Stone Age settlement. For centuries it continued as a farming community, developing into an industrial centre in the Middle Ages. Ragstone, sand and fuller's earth have all been quarried locally; ragstone for building material, sand for glass-making, fuller's earth for the cloth industry. Paper-making and brewing are Maidstone's chief industries today, as they have been since the 17th century.

The Archbishop's Palace south of the High Street is the town's most notable building. Part medieval, part Elizabethan, it was moved to Maidstone from Wrotham and is now a con-ference centre; down by the river are the dungeons in which John Ball was imprisoned until his release by Wat Tyler. In the Archbishop's Stables, across Mill Street, is the Tyrwhitt-Drake Carriage Museum, its exhibits ranging from a 17th-century Italian gig to the Major's coach, all carefully preserved and tended. The exhibitis in Maidstone Museum, housed in an Elizabethan manor in St Faith's Street, are largely connected with Kent over the ages: portraits, costumes, musical instru-ments, together with uniforms and trophies of the Royal West Kent Regiment. In St Peter's Street, which runs parallel with the Medway, is the small chapel of St Peter's, all that remains of a 13th-century hospital for travellers, restored in 1836. Across the river is the College of Priests, established in the 14th century by Archbishop Courtenay at the same time as he built the huge parish church of All Saints, the most opulent in Kent. There are some fine medieval buildings in Bank Street. South of the Ashford Road is Mote Park, a large open space providing facilities for most sports, including sailing on the attractive lake. A mile north of Maidstone is Allington Castle (see above).

Marden, *Kent,* (Tour 4), originally a Roman settlement, for many years it was the main town of the county, with its own Court House, now a shop. It enjoys the distinction of having the Archibishop of Canterbury as its Rector. In the 13th-century church, with its unusual tower is the tombstone of De Luci, Lord Chief Justiciar of Henry II, who drew up the Constitution of Clarendon in 1164 to end the long struggle between Church and State. Beside the church porch are the old village stocks.

Margate, *Kent,* on the north coast of the Isle of Thanet, is the largest seaside resort in the county, with a population of nearly 50 000. Originally a fishing village, it was the invention of the bathing machine by a local Quaker in the 18th century that brought holiday makers and prosperity to the town. Now, with its famous Dreamland amusement park, its bingo halls and fruit machines its car-parks packed with coaches, it has a superficially brash appearance. Yet there is more to Margate than that. There is the 12th-century church of St John's, with its collection of brasses; the Hosking Memorial Museum in the timber-framed Tudor cottage in King Street; the Grotto, a network of underground passages and caves decorated with thousands of sea-shells; and yet more caves in Northdown Road, their chalk walls painted with murals. Margate has a superb sandy beach, and one mile to the east is North Foreland lighthouse, which can be visited on summer afternoons.

Mayfield, *E Sx,* (Tour 8). The church, aloof from the main street was burnt down in a fire in 1389 that destroyed much of the village, so that many of the present buildings date from the 15th century or later. Mayfield College, a Roman Catholic school for girls, is built round the remains of a former palace of the Archbishops of Canterbury; the Great Hall, 70 feet long and 40 feet wide, has survived and is used as a chapel. The first Archbishop to live at Mayfield was St Dunstan, and it was here that he had his famous encounter with the Devil. (See Tunbridge Wells). From Argos Hill, a mile to the northwest, there is a magnificent view across the Weald to Ashdown Forest.

Meopham, *Kent,* pronounced 'Meppam', is 5 miles south of Gravesend on the A227. The triangular green, flanked by two inns and a weather-boarded windmill, has been the venue for cricket matches since 1778. The plan to make Meopham one of London's satellite towns was abandoned, but the village has grown rapidly in recent years.

Mereworth, *Kent,* (pronounced 'Merryworth') is 6 miles west of Maidstone at the junction of the A26 and A228. The first village was demolished by John Fane, later the Earl of Westmorland, to make room for his castle; he then built a new village, complete with church. The castle, with its grey dome and orange walls, is in the Palladian style, with a charming garden. Northwest of the village is the large spread of Mereworth Park.

*****Michelham Priory,** *E Sx,* (Tour 9) stands on the east bank of the Cuckmere River, 2 miles west of Hailsham. Owned by the Sussex Archaeological Trust, the Priory was founded by the Augustinian order in the 13th century on the site of a Norman manor house. Little survives of the original building, which was incorporated into a Tudor farmhouse. The Tudor rooms are faultlessly furnished and contain some fine Dutch paintings and Flemish tapestries. In the gatehouse is the reconstruction of a Sussex forge.

Midhurst, *W Sx,* (Tour 12), is a small town with a wide main street containing attractive Georgian buildings. There are several good hotels, including the Spread Eagle in South Street – a 15th-century coaching inn, and the Angel in North Street. The church is 13th century, restored in the 19th. South of the car-park are the ruins of Cowdray House. Eastward is Cowdray Park (see above).

Midhurst

Minster-in-Thanet, *Kent,* (Tour 1), once a Saxon settlement and a busy port, is a large village with a huge Norman church built on the site of a 7th-century Benedictine abbey. The building was destroyed by Danish raiders in the 10th century, but Minster still has an abbey, a handsome 12th-century manor house established as a Benedictine nunnery in the present century. Part of the house, including the Norman crypt, can be visited.

Newhaven, *E Sx,* is a small cross-Channel and fishing port situated at the mouth of the Ouse between Brighton and Eastbourne, with a population of 10 000. It takes its name from the diversion of the river which, before the storm of 1579, entered the sea at Seaford. The town slopes down to the railway crossing and the harbour, and there is an interesting walk alongside the docks to a small sandy beach by the breakwater. Louis Philippe and his Queen stayed at the 17th-century Bridge Hotel after fleeing from France.

Newington, *Kent,* is a large village on the A2 between Chatham and Sittingbourne, in an area beautiful with white blossom when the cherry trees are out. Thomas à Becket is said to have stayed here on his last and fatal journey to Canterbury. The 13th-century church is a spacious building and contains the shrine of an obscure saint, into the recesses of which cripples used to thrust their legs in the hope of a cure. Outside the church is an ancient pagan sarsen known as the Devil's Stone. Legend has it that the clamour of the church bells so annoyed the Devil that he decided to remove them. However, as he jumped down from the tower he landed on the stone and fell over; the bells rolled out of the sack in which he was carrying them and landed in a stream, which has burbled merrily ever since.

New Romney, *Kent,* (Tour 5), disputes with Dymchurch the title of 'Capital of the Marsh'. Once a harbour, with ships anchoring below the churchyard wall, the town is now more than a mile from the sea. The 12th-century church of St Nicholas, once the meeting place for local government, is one of the finest in the Marsh, its massive tower a landmark for miles around.

*****Newtimber Place,** *W Sx,* (Tour 10), home of his Hon. Judge and Mrs John Clay, is mainly 17th century, with a fine entrance hall, in which the designs on the tapestries and chair coverings match the elaborate frescoes on the walls. The 238 acres of down and woodland on Newtimber Hill, giving views of the Weald and the sea, belong to the National Trust.

North Common, *E Sx,* (Tour 9). North Common, or Chailey Common, is one of the largest in Sussex, a delightful area of heather and gorse and small streams. The main village is south of the common, on the Lewes road. At the northern end of the common, along the A272, are the buildings of Chailey Heritage, a charitable trust started by two social workers from Bermondsey as a home for tubercular East End boys. Now it cares for over 200 physically handicapped children and is administered by the Ministry of Health. A windmill, owned by the Heritage, is said to stand in the dead centre of Sussex. In the northeast corner of the parish is Sheffield Park, see below.

Northiam, *E Sx,* (Tour 5), has a delightful village centre, with a steeply sloping green where Elizabeth I dined under its ancient oak in 1573, leaving her shoes to the village as a memento of her visit. The church, its tall spire rising above the trees, is basically Norman, and there are some fine weather-boarded houses round the green. Northiam's two most important buildings, however, are Brickwall to the south and Great Dixter to the north.

*Brickwall, now a boys' school, takes its name from the high surrounding wall. There is a fine view of the house from the entrance to the grounds. Built of timber and brick in 1633, it presents an imposing front and contains many portraits of the Frewen family, its former owners.

*Great Dixter is a fine example of a large timber-framed hall house, built in the mid 15th century and restored and enlarged by Sir Edwin Lutyens. The great hall is magnificent and unique in its roofing, and among the contents are antique furniture of national importance and needlework dating from the 18th century onward, much of it worked by members of the Lloyd family, who still occupy the house. The gardens, also designed by Lutyens, incorporate many of the old farm buildings and contain a wide variety of unusual plants.

***Nymans,** *W Sx,* (Tour 10) (NT). The house was burnt down in 1947 and only the shell remains, but the garden is one of the finest in the Weald. The centre-piece is a walled garden laid out under the guidance of William Robinson (see West Hoathly) and Gertrude Jekyll; grouped round it are a series of specialized gardens containing rare and beautiful plants, shrubs and trees from all over the world. Illustrated walks are arranged, other than in winter, and refreshments are available.

Offham, *E Sx,* is a small wooded village north of Lewes on the A275. It was on the Downs south of Offham that Simon de Montfort camped with his army on the night of the 13th May 1264, eve of the Battle of Lewes, in which the king's army was soundly defeated. Offham church is mid-Victorian, built to replace the almost inaccessible old church at nearby Hamsey.

Offham, *Kent,* (Tour 6) is a picturesque village with England's last remaining quintain on the green. This medieval apparatus was used in tilting; it is a sort of weather-vane with a weight at one end, the object being to hit the unweighted end with a lance while moving fast enough to avoid being hit by the weight as the quintain swings round.

Oldbury Hill, *Kent,* (NT), is an Iron Age hill-fort of about 100BC, 3 miles southwest of Wrotham on the north side of the A25 and reached from a small lay-by. The site is heavily wooded. In addition to the ramparts, which were probably defended against the Romans around the middle of the 1st century, there are two rock shelters of the middle Palaeolithic period.

*****Old Soar Manor,** *Kent,* (Tour 6), (NT), was a knight's house of the late 13th century and originally belonged to the well-known Culpeper family. The solar, the Lord's private quarters, still survives, together with the chapel and garde-robe, or privy. Next to the solar, on the site of the old hall, is an 18th-century farmhouse, not open to the public.

Otford, *Kent,* once the biggest manor in the county, is on the A225, 2 miles north of Sevenoaks. Despite modern building in the area of the Pilgrim's Way, the centre of the village, with its green, its 12th-century church, its mill and the weeping willows by the pond, is still largely unspoilt. The remains of the Arch-bishops of Canterbury's Tudor palace have been converted into cottages. St Thomas's Well, in a garden near the ruined tower of the palace, is named after Thomas à Becket. According to legend he cursed the nightingale for disturbing his devotions and thumped the ground with his stick; whereupon a spring started to gush and birds ceased to sing in the park.

*****Owl House,** *Kent,* (Tour 4) is a tile-hung house set in 13 acres of spring flowers, azaleas, rhododendrons, roses and rare shrubs, with romantic walks and woodland lakes. 'Owlers' is an old word for smugglers, especially of wool and sheep, and the house, which is not open to the public, was the haunt of smugglers in the 16th century.

Pagham, *W Sx,* situated on the east of Pagham Harbour, is a bungalow town that has merged with Bognor. The Norman church, which contains some interesting stained glass, is dedicated to Thomas à Becket; Becket had a palace here, of which only the moat remains. George V stayed in the parish, at Craigweil House, when convalescent in 1929, although Bognor claims that distinction; hence the king's alleged 'Bugger Bognor' when it was suggested as he lay on his deathbed that he would soon be well enough to visit the resort again. A farmhouse north of Pagham, at Nyetimber, partly pre-Norman and originally a manor, claims to be the oldest house in Sussex that has been continually occupied. In the Middle Ages Pagham Harbour was a port for sea-going vessels. It is now too shallow for all but the smallest craft, and has become a yachting basin and a sanctuary for numerous species of wildfowl and waders.

Parham

*****Parham,** *W Sx,* (Tour 11) is a magnificent greystone mansion set in a vast deer park. Built by Sir Thomas Palmer in 1577, from 1601 to 1922 it was owned by the Bysshop family, and is now the home of Mrs Tritton, grandaughter of the 1st Viscount Cowdray, and her husband. Among the rooms shown to the public are the Great Hall, with its lovely oak screen and Tudor panelling, the 160-foot Long Gallery, the Great Parlour and the Saloon. There are important collections of Elizabethan, Stuart and Georgian portraits, furniture, china, carpets, needlework and tapestries; the 17th-century embroidery on the chairs is amazingly well preserved, and the needlework on the four-post bed in the Great Chamber is traditionally described as having been worked by Mary Queen of Scots.

Patrixbourne, *Kent,* is a delightful village 3 miles southeast of Canterbury in the Nailbourne valley, and believed to be the site of Caesar's defeat of the Britons in the second invasion. Although many of the black-and-white cottages are 19th century they blend happily into the old village scene. The

12th-century church is one of the finest examples of Norman ecclesiastical architecture, with some remarkable stone carving and stained glass.

Pegwell Bay, *Kent,* is on the east coast and one of the coldest spots in the country; in a severe winter the water in the bay often freezes. At low tide its wide expanse of saltings is the haunt of wading birds. On the edge of the bay is an international hoverport, and the Hugin, a replica of a Viking dragon-ship. (See Ebbsfleet.)

**Penshurst, *Kent,* (Tour 7), is one of the most-visited villages in the county. Compact and picturesque, its old houses are an attractive mixture of styles and periods. But it is the great house of the Sidneys and their descendants that attracts the visitors. Massive and solid, Penshurst Place is a Tudor palace built round a 14th-century manor house, surrounded by parkland, orchards and gardens. The splendid Great Hall, with chestnut beams and grotesque carvings, is part of the old manor, and in the crypt below is a collection of arms and armour. Sir Henry Sidney, whose father had been given Penshurst by Edward VI in 1552, added the north and west fronts and the north gatehouse, and on his death it passed to his son Philip – poet, courtier and soldier. His inheritance was shortlived, as he was fatally wounded in the Low Countries when he was only 32. Philip's brother Robert, later the Earl of Leicester, extended the house southward with the Long and Nether galleries; and when the male line died out in the 18th century the estate passed to Sir John Shelley, who added the name of Sidney to his own. It was Sir John Shelley and his successors, the Lords de L'Isle and Dudley, who carried out the final work of restoration and rebuilding.

Penshurst is full of beautiful furniture and tapestries. Pictures adorn the walls, and at the rear of the house is a Toy Museum. The Sidney chapel is in the village church, where most of the family are buried; Sir Philip Sidney, however, is missing. He was buried in St Paul's.

**Petworth, *W Sx,* (Tour 12) (NT), stands on a hill at the junction of 5 main roads and is one of the most picturesque small towns in Sussex, although its narrow winding streets were not built to cope with the volume of traffic they now have to carry. Two great families dominate the history of the town: the Percys, Dukes of Northumberland, and the Wyndhams, Earls of Egremont. It was the 3rd Earl of Egremont who built the 18th-century stone town hall in the market square. The 14th-

century church was restored in 1827 but the spire, a prominent landmark, was demolished as unsafe in 1947. In the north aisle of the church is a statue of the 3rd Earl, sculpted by Edward Bailey, who also did the figure at the top of Nelson's column. Below the tower is a monument to the Percys, erected in 1837.

Petworth came to the Percys in the 12th century, through the marriage of Josceline de Louvaine to Agnes Percy. In 1670 it passed to the Dukes of Somerset and finally to the Wyndhams. It was the 6th Duke of Somerset who built Petworth House, late in the 17th century; over 300 feet long, the house is set in a beautiful deer park landscaped by Capability Brown. The largest of the state rooms was decorated by Grinling Gibbons with a profusion of limewood carvings; there are Laguerre murals from top to bottom of the Grand Staircase and a fine book collection in the White Library. The North Gallery was specially built to house the magnificent collection of sculpture, and there are paintings everywhere, from Vandyke to Turner. Turner spent much time at Petworth, painting the house and the park and fishing in the lake.

***Pevensey,** *E Sx,* (Tour 8) is a village full of history. William of Normandy landed here in 1066, and although Pevensey had been an important port before that its importance now increased. It had its own mint where the 14th-century Mint House, a present-day antique shop, now stands, and its own Court House, now a museum. But over the years the harbour silted up, and Pevensey now is nearly a mile inland from Pevensey Bay, a holiday resort of beach huts and bungalows. *Pevensey Castle* was built by the Romans around 280 as one of the forts of the Saxon Shore (see Richborough); the Roman walls are reasonably well preserved, with an impressive West Gateway. When the Normans came they built their castle in the southeast corner, and much of the inner bailey survives, including the keep and the later gatehouse. It withstood sieges by both William Rufus and Simon de Montfort, and housed a gun emplacement during the Second World War. The castle is reputed to be haunted by the ghost of Andrew Borde, court physician and unofficial jester to Henry VIII, who lived in the Mint House and died in the Fleet Prison, where he was imprisoned for debt. The Mint House too is haunted, by the ghost of a 16th-century woman who was starved to death in a locked room by her lover after he had found her in bed with another man. Before locking her up, however, he cut out her tongue and forced her to watch her paramour being roasted to death.

Pilgrims' Way, *Kent,* which runs from Winchester to Canterbury through Hampshire, Surrey and Kent, is something of a misnomer, for the route was originally trodden in Neolithic times, as the great tombs of Addington, Coldrum and Kit's Coty bear witness. Hilaire Belloc preferred to call it the Old Road. But because it was there, travellers down the ages continued to use it, and the Romans even built their villas along it. Almost certainly the pilgrims must have used it, travelling westward to St Swithun's shrine at Winchester, eastward to St Thomas's at Canterbury. Except where it passes through private estates, as at Chevening northwest of Sevenoaks, most of it can be followed today; partly on metalled lanes, partly on well-defined tracks. Entering Kent a mile northwest of Westerham, it runs roughly parallel to the A25, through Otford, Kemsing and Trottiscliffe (Tour 6) to Paddlesworth. Here the pilgrims could either take the ferry over the Medway to Burham or go north to cross it by the bridge at Rochester; and of those who chose the latter alternative some would have continued on to Canterbury along the Roman Watling Street. Others, however, would have returned to pick up the Old Road at Burham. This now turns southeast through Boxley, Detling and Hollingbourne (Tour 3) to Boughton Lees, and from there northeast through Chilham (Tour 2) to Canterbury.

Plaistow, *W Sx,* (Tour 11) is an isolated village, well away from main roads in wooded country. The green is attractive, with magnificent oaks in the centre and a good view across to the South Downs. A stunted tree is said to have been that planted by Nell Gwyn while she was staying at the 16th-century Plaistow Place.

Plaxtol, *Kent,* (Tour 6) stands high up with the inn and the forge, now a restaurant, at the crossroads. There too is the church, exceptional in having been built during the Civil War. At the bottom of the hill is Spout House, a medieval building housing a museum of ironwork. Along the road towards Shipbourne is Fairlawne Park, formerly the home of the Vane family; a Vane was governor of Massachusetts, and another was executed on Tower Hill and his headless body buried in the church crypt. Christopher Smart, the poet, who spent many years in Bedlam and died in the King's Bench Prison after being arrested for debt, was born in Fairlawne, where his father was steward. A mile east of Plaxtol is Old Soar Manor (see above).

Pluckley, *Kent,* (Tour 4) is situated on a ridge 5 miles northwest of Ashford, with a fine view over the Beult plain. Long associated with the Dering family, there is Dering Farm and Dering Wood to the south and Surrenden Dering to the east. It has been described as the most haunted village in England.

Ramsgate, *Kent,* is a large seaside resort on the Isle of Thanet, with an outer harbour for fishing boats and an inner harbour and marina for smaller craft, the harbours protected by piers. There are some attractive Georgian crescents on the cliffs and a model Tudor village. St Lawrence, the old parish church supported by massive Norman pillars, is at the top of the High Street, with the present Victorian parish church at the bottom. The Catholic church of St Augustine was the work of Augustus Pugin, a convert from Protestantism. Built in 1842 from his fees as an architect, Pugin ran out of money before the intended spire could be added to the tower. He died in 1852 and is buried in the churchyard. Karl Marx used to stay in Ramsgate and Van Gogh taught languages here before turning to painting as a career. West of the town is Pegwell Bay (see above).

Reculver, *Kent,* is 3½ miles east of Herne Bay on the north coast, and largely a caravan township. The square military fortress was built by the Romans for coastal defence against the Saxons, and in the 7th century King Egbert built a church in the centre. Twin towers were added in the 12th century and were known to seamen as 'The Sisters'. In the 19th century the church fell into disrepair and was vandalized, but Trinity House saved it from complete destruction and maintained the remains as a guide to shipping.

Richborough Castle, *Kent,* (Tour 1), was the first and greatest fortress built by the Romans in England and the centre of one of the most populated areas. The walls were up to 12 feet thick, with interior walls separating the various rooms of the community. Although much has now vanished, in places the flint and stone walls are 25 feet high, laced with the red tiles typical of Roman construction. In the centre of the castle are the foundations of a vast monument, built in the form of a cross. A small museum displays relics found on the site.

Rochester, *Kent,* is a city rich in history. It was here that King Alfred built the first English navy. It was an important Roman town on the Dover to London road and the Normans, recognizing its strategic value, built one of their strongest fortresses to dominate it. There has been a bridge over the Medway here since Saxon times. A stone bridge, built in 1387, lasted for nearly 500 years and was then replaced.

On a mound above the bridge stand cathedral and castle, side by side. The original Saxon cathedral was largely destroyed by Danish invaders and the Norman building that replaced it was damaged by fire on several occasions and by Cromwell's soldiers during the Civil War. The lovely west front, with its great Norman door, is the best of the exterior. The castle, begun in 1087, was not finished until nearly 50 years later; its massive keep, nearly 130 feet high with walls 12 feet thick, towers above the town. The castle was besieged several times, the most spectacular occasion being in 1215, when it was seized by rebel barons. King John had his sappers dig a tunnel under a corner of the keep and prop it with timber. He then arranged for 'forty pigs of the fattest and those less good for eating' to be killed, pushed into the tunnel and set alight. As the timber burned the earth above collapsed, bringing down that corner of the keep to provide an entry for the King's men.

There is much to see in addition to the castle and the cathedral, including the flourishing dockyard and the Bridge Chamber used by the wardens who regulate the traffic across the river to Chatham. Behind the castle keep is the timbered Old Hall, where Henry VIII met Anne of Cleves on her arrival in England. Across the Maidstone road is the redbrick Restoration House, where Charles II stayed on his way back to London from exile and the fictional home of Dickens' Miss Haversham; Dickens, who loved Rochester, spent his boyhood across the river in Chatham (see above), and many of its buildings play a part in his novels. The High Street is rich in ancient buildings: the Corn Exchange and the 17th-century Guildhall; the Victorian precinct of La Providence, originally 17th-century almshouses; the Royal Victoria and Bull hotel, (the Bull in *Pickwick Papers*), and many old shop fronts. In the High Street too is the Eastgate House Museum, a Tudor mansion devoted largely to the history of Rochester and to Dickens (see Gads Hill).

The Romney, Hythe and Dymchurch Railway, *Kent,* which opened in 1927, is the longest miniature steam railway in the world, with a track laid to a gauge of 15 inches that runs for nearly 14 miles from Hythe to Dungeness, with Dymchurch, St Mary's Bay and New Romney the principal intermediate stations. Operating on a regular schedule, with an increased service during the high season, the railway's 11 locomotives are roughly one-third size versions of famous main line expresses of the 1920s and 1930s, and in its 70 carriages it carries more than 300 000 passengers a year. The route traverses the rich farmland of Romney Marsh, the fields crowded with sheep and intersected by waterways, and provides a splendid view of the coast, with its magnificent beaches still defended by Martello towers.

Romney Marsh, *Kent,* (Tour 5) is the name commonly used to describe the area that stretches along the coast from Hythe to the Sussex border and inland as far as Tenterden, although in fact Romney Marsh proper extends westward only as far as New Romney, the rest of the area consisting of Walland Marsh and the Rother and other Levels. It is well-drained pasture-land, famous for its black-nosed sheep. For the inhabitants there has always been a constant battle against the sea. The Romans built the great embankments known as the Dym-church Wall and the Rhee Wall, but these did not prevent the great storms at the end of the 13th century from building up a shingle bank that changed the course of the Rother, so that it reached the sea at Rye instead of at New Romney.

The marsh is a remote, rather insular region, windswept and inhospitable and sparsely populated, with little to attract industry or the developer. The coast is an exception. Here there are car-parks, holiday camps and chalets, with the light-houses and atomic power station at Dungeness. Richard Barham wrote in the *Ingoldsby Legends* that 'the world, according to the best geographers, is divided into Europe, Asia, Africa, America and Romney Marsh', and it was because of its remoteness that the Marshmen in the past became notorious as wreckers and smugglers, for the marsh was a region the excisemen were reluctant to enter. The Marshmen also enjoyed a certain amount of independence, and until as late as 1950 a local government body known as the Lords of the Level exercised considerable power.

Rotherfield, *E Sx,* is a pleasant village 7 miles south of Tunbridge Wells on the B2100. Situated in hilly and wooded country, it looks westward to Ashdown Forest. A Saxon land-owner built the first church in the 8th century, dedicating it to St Denys after he had been cured at a monastery of that name near Paris. He also established a monastery here, probably near the church, although nothing of it remains. The present church is 12th century with later additions. It contains some fine wood-carvings, and an 18th-century painting of the village showing ruins that could have been those of the old Saxon monastery.

Rottingdean, *E Sx,* is a small coastal town 3½ miles east of
Brighton, situated in a break in the cliffs and once the haunt of

smugglers. The old part of the town lies inland, with a green and a village pond and the church nearby; villagers who had taken refuge in the church belfry during a French raid in 1377 were burned to death when it was set on fire. The artist Burne-Jones lived by the green and is buried in the churchyard. Lady Burne-Jones was Rudyard Kipling's aunt, and before moving to Bateman's (see under Burwash) in 1902 Kipling also lived in Rottingdean, at The Elms; it was here that he wrote *Kim* and the *Stalky* stories, among others. Here too lived the artist Sir William Nicholson, whose house, The Grange, is now a museum. A mile along the coast road to Brighton is Roedean, a girls' public school.

*Royal Greenwich Observatory, *E Sx,* (Tour 8) is at Herstmonceux Castle. Built by Roger de Fiennes in the mid 15th century to defend the Pevensey Levels, the castle was one of the first large brick-buildings in England since Roman times, although with its turrets and battlements and surrounded by a moat its design is similar to other castles of its age. During the 18th century it fell into decay and was largely dismantled, and was only restored to its present perfection during this century In 1957 it was taken over by the Royal Observatory, who moved here from Greenwich. Although the castle is not open to the public, the gardens, formal in design and beautifully kept, may be visited in the summer. Visitors may also inspect the Isaac Newton telescope, the largest in Britain, and a replica of one of Newton's own telescopes.

Royal Greenwich Observatory, Herstmonceux

Rye, *E Sx,* (Tour 5), at the head of the Rother estuary, was once a busy port; but the great storm of 1287 washed away a large part of the town and nearly a century later the French completed its destruction. Now, built on a hill, it is one of the most picturesque little towns in the southeast, with crooked cobbled streets and some beautiful half-timbered and Georgian buildings. There are numerous old inns, among them the Mermaid and the Flushing, both dating from the 16th century. The Ypres Tower, a 12th-century castle, now a museum, contains a fine collection of pottery; the 400-year-old clock of St Mary's Church on Lion Street is believed to be the oldest church clock in England still with its original works. *Lamb House* (NT), is probably the most famous building in Rye. It is a beautiful Georgian house built by James Lamb, one-time mayor of Rye and the subject of a murder attempt that went astray; the assassin, John Breede, was hanged after killing Lamb's brother-in-law by mistake, and his skull can be seen in the Town Hall. Lamb House is perhaps more famous as the home of the American writer Henry James, who lived there from 1897 until 1914. A room in the house is preserved as a Henry James museum.

*St John's Jerusalem, *Kent,* (NT) is an old moated house at Sutton-at-Hone, 3 miles south of Dartford on the east side of the A225. Once the property of the Knights Hospitallers, where Henry III often stayed, it was bought in 1665 by Abraham Hill, Treasurer of the Royal Society, who rebuilt it. It was further improved by Edward Hasted, the Kent historian, in the 18th century, but the walls and the former chapel are now all that remains. The grounds, comprising 45½ acres, contain a weeping willow descended from the tree under which Napoleon was buried, and other historic trees.

St Leonards, *E Sx,* is a seaside resort on the south coast adjacent to Hastings. It dates from 1828 and was built around the Royal Victoria Hotel to form a select residential area away from its neighbour. Later development has largely defeated the purpose, although the town still manages to retain an exclusive air. The church was destroyed by a flying bomb in 1944 and rebuilt 17 years later.

St Margaret's-at-Cliffe, *Kent,* is situated 3 miles northeast of Dover. Here, as in St Margaret's Bay at the bottom of the steep hill, are holiday camps and caravan sites, guest houses and hotels and car-parks – everything for the seaside visitor. The church is splendid, built of Caen stone and almost totally Norman, with a fine west doorway; in smuggling times the belfry was used as a store for contraband goods. South of the bay is Lighthouse Down, 9 acres of land on the South Foreland, acquired by the National Trust in 1978 and providing a pleasant walk along the cliffs. Kingsdown Lees north of the bay is also National Trust property, with an obelisk commemorating the work of the Dover Patrol in two world wars.

St-Mary-in-the-Marsh, *Kent,* (Tour 5) is a small, remote village. E Nesbit, author of children's poems and stories, lived here in two disused Army huts and is buried in the churchyard, her grave marked by a barge-board inscribed by her husband. A tablet in the lovely church commemorates the centenary of her birth in 1858.

Saltwood, *Kent,* (Tour 2), an attractive village on the outskirts of Hythe, derives its name from the practice of using wood to boil off the seawater in the saltpans along the shore. Here are the creeper-clad ruins of Saltwood Castle, home of the Clark family, where the murderers of Thomas à Becket met before setting out for Canterbury. As Archbishop, Becket previously owned the castle, and the present library was his Audience Hall. The main residence is now in the Great Gateway. Parts of the outer buildings of the castle may be seen in the summer by previous arrangement.

Sandgate, *Kent,* is a westward extension of Folkestone. On the beach is Sandgate Castle, built on the same ground plan as those at Deal and Walmer by Henry VIII. It was repaired and altered during the Napoleonic Wars, but exposure to the sea has reduced it almost to a ruin. H G Wells lived at Sandgate, at Spade House, in a steep street above the sea, near the lovely terraced garden of Radnor Cliff House. Inland from the town is Shorncliff camp, with its large redbrick garrison church.

Sandwich, *Kent,* (Tour 1), is one of the Cinque Ports, although 1½ miles inland from the east coast. Originally a Saxon port, by the mid 15th century it had become an important naval base; yet 100 years later the harbour was silting up, and a petition to Elizabeth I, presented to her when she stayed at the timbered Old House in 1573, failed to get it cleared. The decline of the harbour, however, saw Sandwich develop as a cloth-making centre, with weavers brought over from the Low Countries. The Weavers, one of the most attractive old houses in the town, is still connected with the craft.

It is wisest to explore Sandwich on foot, for traffic congestion can be bad. There are the old town walls, with the medieval Fisher Gate and the 16th-century Barbican. The Tudor Guildhall in the market square houses the old courtroom; above is the council chamber, its walls hung with paintings, and a museum on the top floor. St Clement's is the finest of the three medieval churches, enlarged over the centuries; St Mary's was damaged by an earthquake in the 16th century, and 100 years later the tower collapsed, as did that of St Peter's. Outside the town wall is the medieval hospital of St Bartholomew, with a lovely 13th-century chapel. There are three fine golf courses along the dunes, and Sandwich Bay has an excellent sandy beach. Northwest of the town a lane off the A257 leads to Richborough Castle (see above).

Sedlescombe, *E Sx,* (Tour 8), where Titus Oates went to school, is a picturesque village, with houses, tea-rooms and antique shops spreading up the hill on either side of the narrow green. The large church is at the north end of the village, a 17th-century seating plan revealing how the niceties of social status were observed.
* *Pestalozzi Children's Village,* which can be visited by appointment, is at the south end of Sedlescombe. Named after a Swiss educationalist who cared for orphans during the Napoleonic Wars, it is an offshoot of the original Swiss village at Trogen, founded after the Second World War. Opened in 1959, the Sedlescombe village was a home for children from displaced persons camps in Europe, each nationality having its own cedarwood home and retaining its customs. Nowadays it is largely a training centre for children from the developing countries.

Selsey, *W Sx,* is a seaside town situated at the toe of Selsey Peninsula, a flat area south of Chichester, popular with holiday makers. The town has a long main street leading to the front, where high sea-walls protect the houses from the pounding of the sea. There is a good beach, but no promenade for cars.
Selsey Peninsula has a long history. Vespasian landed here. So, 400 years later, did the Saxon Aella, to begin his invasion of Sussex. The peninsula was given to Wilfred, Bishop of York and the patron saint of Sussex, by King Aethelwalch, and much of it is still church property. The southern coastline is constantly changing, the sea inundating parts and retreating from others. An ancient cathedral, abandoned in the 11th century in favour of Chichester, stood on land now covered by the sea, and blocks of the Caen stone with which it was built are occasionally found on the shore.

Sevenoaks, *Kent,* (Tour 6) has a population of nearly 20 000, many of whom commute daily to London. The present buildings of Sevenoaks School, flanked by almshouses, were designed early in the 17th century by Lord Burlington, although the school had existed for at least 300 years before that. Opposite the school is the tall 13th-century church, much restored, where John Donne, the poet, was rector early in the 17th century. Among some attractive old buildings is the Red House, once the home of Jane Austen's uncle.

Knowle (NT), however, is the most splendid house in Sevenoaks, being one of the largest private houses in England: a vast complex of buildings and courtyards, with stone towers and fortress-like walls. Begun in 1456, in 1566 Elizabeth I gave it to her cousin, Thomas Sackville, 1st Earl of Dorset, who greatly extended it. The State Rooms, grouped around the Stone Court, contain a large collection of pictures, rare furniture, rugs and tapestries which present a spectacle of ancient splendour unique in Europe. In the Great Hall is a magnificent carved oak screen, and there are huge four-post beds in all the bedrooms, that in the King's Bedroom decorated with ostrich plumes. Herds of deer roam the 1000-acre park of grass and woodland, and on the south side of the house is the curious cottage that Vita Sackville-West claimed to have given her nightmares in her childhood.

*Sheffield Park, *E Sx,* (Tour 9) (NT). The park gardens, laid out by Capability Brown 200 years ago, are one of the glories of Sussex, with rare trees and magnificent shrubs, lawns and glades surrounding four lakes; the rhododendrons and azaleas are particularly fine. At one time the park contained one of the finest private cricket grounds in the country, and many famous cricketers have played there. Edward Gibbon, author of *The Decline and Fall of the Roman Empire* and close friend of the first Earl, often stayed at the house. At the cross-roads north of the park is the Sheffield Arms, an imposing Georgian building.

Sheppey, Isle of, *Kent,* is off the north coast, connected to the mainland by the magnificent Kingsferry Bridge over the Swale, built in 1960 to replace an older bridge. Sheppey means 'sheep island', and there are still sheep grazing in the low-lying marshy meadows ribbed with inlets and waterways. Towns and industry are concentrated in the northwest corner of the island, with a number of holiday camps along the coast. In the centre, at Eastchurch, is one of H M prisons.

Shipley, *W Sx,* (Tour 10). Although only a short distance from the busy A272 it remains serene and undisturbed. Hilaire Belloc lived here, in King's Land, and it was Belloc who began the restoration of Shipley Mill, one of the biggest smock mills in the country. He died in 1953 before the work was finished, but it was completed later and is now the only working mill in West Sussex. The lovely 12th-century church, built by the Knights Templar, contains the Shipley reliquary, a 12th-century wooden casket decorated with Limoges enamel and probably a gift from the Templars; also in the church is the magnificent monument to Sir Thomas Caryll and his wife, dated 1616. In the churchyard is the grave of John Ireland, the composer.

Shoreham, *Kent,* (Tour 6), is a peaceful village on the Darent. The 15th-century flint church, from where there is a delightful riverside walk to Shoreham Castle Farm, has a splendid timbered porch, and a door carved from a single oak, together with a rood-screen that is probably the finest in the county; from the churchyard there is a view of the chalk cross cut in the slope of the Downs in memory of those killed in the 1914-18 war. Several famous people have been associated with Shoreham, notably General Ireton, the painter Samuel Palmer, and the poets William Blake and Lord Dunsany.

Shoreham by Sea, *W Sx,* is 6 miles west of Brighton. For 1500 years there has been a harbour here, and in medieval times it was one of the busiest along the Channel coast. The modern harbour is still important, protected by a two-mile finger of land running parallel to the coast. The present parish church of St Mary de Haura ('of the harbour') has a magnificent tower, with four equally magnificent arches below; St Nicholas, the old parish church, has a Saxon nave and a wooden screen across the chancel that is one of the oldest in the country. Marlipins, a 12th-century stone-and-flint building and the old toll house, is now a museum. Two miles northeast of the town is Shoreham Gap, 596 acres of downland belonging to the National Trust.

***Sissinghurst Castle,** *Kent,* (Tour 4) (NT) is situated midway between Tunbridge Wells and Ashford, off the A262. Originally a Tudor manor house belonging to the Baker family, whose most notorious member was Sir John Baker, known as 'Bloody Baker' (see Cranbrook), in the mid 18th century it was used to house French prisoners of war, who vandalized it; later it became a poorhouse and was eventually pulled down, leaving only the tower. But it is the castle gardens that make Sissinghurst exceptional. In 1930 it became the home of Sir Harold Nicholson and his wife, better known as Vita Sackville-

West, and over the years they created one of the most beautiful and romantic gardens in Kent. In the tower is Lady Nicholson's study, furnished as she left it and containing photographs showing house and gardens in their various stages of transformation.

Sittingbourne, *Kent,* is a busy town on the A2; modern, yet with claims to antiquity. North of the main road is the industrial area, with its wharves and timber-yards and paper-mills, and the Dolphin Sailing Barge Museum, open at week-ends. To the south are the residential and administrative buildings, and the lime-lined Avenue of Remembrance commemorating Sittingbourne men killed in the First World War. The roof of the 13th-century church was repaired in the 18th century after being destroyed by fire by careless workmen.

Slindon, *W Sx,* (Tour 11) is a pleasant village extending up the southern slope of the Downs with several 17th-century flint cottages and the village square at the top. Slindon House was originally a palace of the Archbishops of Canterbury, and in the 12th-century church is a tablet to Stephen Langton, who died at Slindon in 1228; there is also a wooden effigy, unique in Sussex, of Sir Anthony St Leger, who asked to be buried there. The Slindon Estate, including Slindon Park, which is open to the public, is owned by the National Trust and is crossed by nearly 4 miles of the Roman Stane Street (see below).

****Smallhythe Place,** *Kent,* (Tour 5) (NT), was the home of the actress Ellen Terry for 30 years until her death in 1928. A 15th-century yeoman's house, built for the harbourmaster when Small Hythe was a ship-building centre and port, it is now a museum and contains the relics of Ellen Terry and other famous stage personalities. The barn theatre and Priest's House cannot be visited.

Smarden, *Kent,* 8 miles due west of Ashford on the B2077, is one of the many lovely Wealden villages, the tiled and weatherboarded houses jostling each other in picturesque fashion. The church is 14th century, with a wide nave spanned by a roof of intersecting timbers and sometimes called the Barn of Kent.

Sompting, *W Sx,* is just south of the A27, 1½ miles from Worthing, with the parish church of St Mary's across the main road. St Mary's has been described as one of the treasures of England. The body of the church was pulled down by the Knights Templar in the 12th century and rebuilt, but they retained the Saxon tower, which is nearly 1000 years old. The tower roof is practically unique in this country; known as a 'Rhenish helm', it consists of four diamond-shaped surfaces meeting at a point. The original entrance to the church was through the main porch of the tower, now marked by a splendid Saxon arch, into the west end of the nave. The modern entrance is into the south transept, which in the 12th century was the Templars' private chapel, separate from the rest of the church. The Templars also built two small chapels, which now form the north transept; but in 1306 they were expelled from the church and replaced by the Knights Hospitallers, who opened the Templars' private chapel to the parishioners and built their own chapel on the northwest side of the nave. This fell into decay, but a room was built on the site in 1971. Other items of interest are the Saxon carvings on the walls, an Easter sepulchre in the chancel, and at the lych gate a coffin resting by the village War Memorial.

Speldhurst, *Kent,* (Tour 7) is a neat hilltop village, whose half-timbered George and Dragon Inn is one of the oldest in the county, possibly early 13th century. St Mary's church was struck by lightning in the 18th century and rebuilt early in the 19th, with some fine stained-glass windows designed by Burne-Jones.

***Standen,** W Sx,* (Tour 7) (NT). Built in 1894, it is the only major house designed by Philip Webb to remain untouched, containing period furniture and a good collection of pictures and pottery. The wallpaper and textiles were designed by William Morris. From the attractive hillside garden there are fine views across the Medway valley.

Stane Street, *W Sx,* is the old Roman road, the only one crossing Sussex, that ran from Chichester to London over the Downs and across the western Weald, passing through Halnaker, Pulborough (a Roman garrison town), Billingshurst and into Surrey. The modern A29 follows much the same route. The section of Stane Street through the Slindon Estate and Earthem Woods up to Bignor is particularly well preserved.

Stanmer, *E Sx,* is a downland village on the outskirts of Brighton, reached by a turning off the A27 and little more than a solitary street which goes nowhere. The church is practically a receptacle for memorials to the Pelham family, the Earls of Chichester, who owned Stanmer Park until it was bought by

Brighton Corporation. The park is open to the public and the gardens are used as a nursery. The house is now part of the University of Sussex.

Staplehurst, *Kent,* (Tour 4). On a main road and a main railway line, it has inevitably attracted commuters, and the modern buildings do not all merge kindly with the old. The church register is one of the earliest in the country to be written on paper instead of the usual parchment. A stone column commemorates the death of three female martyrs, burnt at the stake in Canterbury.

Steyning, *W Sx,* (Tour 10), pronounced 'Stenning', is an attractive small town, and the many antique and tea-shops are a measure of the number of visitors it receives. Until the Adur silted up in the 14th century it was, like its neighbour Bramber, an important port, and a royal manor with its own mint. The splendid 12th-century church, a miniature cathedral with a quantity of Norman moulding, stands on the site of a timbered Saxon church; a broken Saxon coffin lid, now displayed in the porch, strengthens the belief that Ethelwulf, father of King Alfred, was buried in the churchyard. The 15th-century grammar school was originally the home of a religious community.

Church Street, Steyning

Sundridge, *Kent,* (Tour 6), is a Domesday village. Combe Bank, now a girls' school, a white Georgian mansion with a splendidly decorated library, once belonged to the Duke of Argyll, whose son, Lord Ferrers, was the last peer of England to be hanged. Sundridge Old Hall, a typical Kentish yeoman's house, was built about 1458 and belongs to the National Trust. 85

Just over a mile north of the village is Chevening Place, built by Inigo Jones early in the 17th century and once the home of the eccentric Stanhope family. The Pilgrims' Way passes through Chevening Park, but the 3rd Earl persuaded Parliament to bring in an Enclosure Act to stop travellers using it. The house was left in trust by the 7th Earl, to be occupied by members of the royal family or other exalted personages.

Swanscombe, *Kent,* 3 miles east of Dartford, is famous for the discovery of a skull which is accepted as being that of a prehistoric man or woman; worked flints and relics of animals long extinct in Britain have also been found. In the flint-built church, badly damaged by lightning in 1902, is the fine Jacobean tomb of Sir Ralph Weldon, with the knight raised on an elbow to gaze tenderly down on his wife and children.

Tenterden, *Kent,* (Tour 5), vies with Cranbrook for the title of 'Capital of the Weald'. Once a wool town and harbour, it is now a small market town and shopping centre with some fine buildings, both public and private. A High Street inn

Tenterden

commemorates the name of William Caxton, pioneer of printing, whom the town claims as a former citizen. The church of St Mildred's has a splendid pinnacled tower from which was hung the beacon that warned of the approach of the Spanish Armada.

Thanet, Isle of, *Kent,* (Tour 1), forms the northeast corner of the county, separated from the mainland by the Wantsum Channel – once an important sea-lane, now little more than a weed-infested ditch. Thanet is said to have the most bracing air in Kent, and the coast, with its steep white cliffs, is almost one continuous holiday resort. Inland the terrain is high and flat and treeless, with vast fields largely planted with potatoes.

Tonbridge, *Kent,* bypassed by the A21 to relieve the former congestion in the High Street, is an ancient town best known for its public school and its castle. The castle stands on the motte of a former Saxon fort overlooking the Medway; built in the reign of Henry I, its great gateway on the landward side, with flanking towers, is the most striking of the remaining buildings. The site, pleasantly landscaped with lawns and flowerbeds, is in the care of the local council, who have their offices in a Georgian mansion beside the gatehouse. Tonbridge School was founded in 1553 by Sir Andrew Judd, Lord Mayor of London and Master of the Skinners Company. The present buildings are mainly mid Victorian, with an imposing brick chapel added in 1902. The school can be visited on application to the porter's lodge. Other buildings of note are the 16th-century Chequers Hotel in the High Street and the Port Reeve's house in East Street. Industries include printing and the manufacture of cricket balls, and down by the river there are sawmills and timber wharves.

Trottiscliffe, *Kent,* (Tour 6), pronounced 'Trosley', is a small village whose church has an enormous pulpit, reputed to have come from Westminster Abbey, and contains a collection of human and animal bones found at nearby Coldrum (see above). Graham Sutherland, the artist, used to live here.

Trotton, *W Sx,* 4 miles west of Midhurst on the A272, the village has a lovely 5-arched bridge over the western Rother, built in the 15th century by Lord Camoys, a veteran of Agincourt. The church of St George has a 14th-century wall painting of the Last Supper and two magnificent Camoys brasses, one of them the only known brass to a woman in this country. In the past the village was noted for its archers, and grooves on a door jamb were probably caused by the sharpening of arrows.

Tunbridge Wells, *Kent,* (Tour 7) is the only wholly post-medieval town in the county. It owes its existence to the discovery in 1606 of the chalybeate spring by Lord North, who took a sample of the water back to London. 'The Wells' soon became a popular summer resort for members of Charles I's court, and in 1630 Queen Henrietta came there to recuperate after the birth of the future Charles II. The town reached its peak as a fashionable resort during the Regency period, and was granted the title of Royal by Edward VII in 1909.

The spring is in the Pantiles, a pedestrian precinct named after the large roofing tiles with which it was paved. Legend has

it that St Dunstan was working at his forge in Mayfield when
the Devil appeared to tempt him, disguised as a beautiful
young woman. Noticing the hooves beneath the skirt, St
Dunstan seized the Devil by the nose with red-hot pincers;
whereupon the Devil returned to his natural form and flew off
to plunge his nose in a spring at Mayfield and then in the one at
Tunbridge Wells, thereby giving both springs their chalybeate
qualities. Near the Pantiles is the church of St Charles the
Martyr, built after the Restoration, its rather disappointing
exterior hiding riches within, including a splendidly-decorated
plaster ceiling.

From here the main part of the town stretches northward,
with the High Street rising steeply to Mount Pleasant and the
multi-storied car-park and the houses and shrubberies of
Calverley Park; off the High Street cobbled alleyways of small
18th-century houses lead up to Mount Sion. The common, with
its trees and bracken and outcrops of rock, is detached from the
town and yet part of it, with the big hotels along Mount
Ephraim at the top. Westward are the High Rocks which,
although nowhere more than 50 feet high, are of such a variety
of shapes that they are used as a training ground for would-be
climbers. Few people now visit Tunbridge Wells expressly to
take the waters. But it has beauty and charm and is one of the
finest shopping centres in the southeast.

Uckfield, *E Sx,* is a busy little town on the A26, 8 miles north of
Lewes, with a population of around 7 500. Originally a hamlet
dependent on neighbouring Buxted, it grew up with the coming
of the railway. A long hill forms the High Street, a good
shopping centre, with the Maiden's Head, a large Georgian
inn, near the top. Further down is the ancient Olive's Yard. At
the bottom of the hill, near the railway station, are Bridge
Cottages, which date from 1380. The church has a 15th-century
tower, with an enormous cedar in the churchyard.

***Uppark,** *W Sx,* (Tour 12) (NT), is a beautiful 17th-century
house set in woodland high on the Downs below South Harting, with a magnificent view across rolling country to the sea
and the Isle of Wight. Sir Matthew Fetherstonhaugh, who
bought the house in 1747 along with the manors of South and
East Harting, died in 1774, and six years later his only son
Harry brought the lovely Emma Hart, a fifteen year old 'show-
girl' with a baby on her hands, to live with him. He tired of her a
year later and sent her packing, giving her no more than the
fare to her grandmother's home. But poverty was not to be
Emma's lot. She was befriended by Charles Greville, who had

met her at Uppark, and later married Sir William Hamilton and became Nelson's mistress.

The way up to the house is steep, through luxuriant woodland. When, after Waterloo, Uppark was offered to the Duke of Wellington by a grateful nation, he wrote to Sir Harry that 'from all I have heard and know of Uppark I should prefer to have that place to any other', but on visiting it he changed his mind, deciding that the hill would be too hard on his horses. It is not hard on a car, however, and opposite the gate of the house is a clearing in the woods where one can park and eat a picnic meal.

Uppark was built about 1690 and owes much to Humphrey Repton, the famous landscape gardener, who made several improvements to the house and grounds at the beginning of the 19th century. The rooms are full of beautiful furniture, porcelain and pictures, most of it 17th or 18th century, with the original wallpaper and curtains. In the service lobby is the Uppark dolls' house, miraculously preserved; the furniture Queen Anne, the vessels of hallmarked silver, glass or pewter and every doll exquisitely dressed. The kitchen quarters provide a fascinating insight into life below stairs in early Victorian times. In the garden is the Gothick summer house, and an elegant little dairy at the end of the west terrace.

Wadhurst, *E Sx,* (Tour 8) was once a centre of the iron industry, and the church floor is largely paved with iron graveslabs; the iron candlesticks and cross on the altar are modern. Wadhurst was the scene of the last important prize fight in England, held in December 1863.

*****Wakehurst Place,** *W Sx,* (Tour 10) (NT), is a Tudor mansion formerly owned by the Culpepers, a family whose name crops up constantly in the southeast. In the 476 acres of gardens and woodland there is an important collection of exotic trees, shrubs and other plants, the trees labelled as at Kew. It is administered by the Director of the Royal Botanic Gardens at Kew.

Walmer, *Kent,* now one with Deal and roughly equal to it in population, is famous mainly for its castle, the largest and most southerly of the 'Three castles that keep the Downs'. (See Deal). Completed by 1540, its defences were never tested and early in the 18th century it became the official residence of the Lords Warden of the Cinque Ports, with windows cut in the walls, living rooms added to the fortifications and a garden laid out. The Duke of Wellington died in the castle while in office, and his room is as he left it. William Pitt's study still contains some of his furniture. Castle apart, Walmer has its own particular charm, with some attractive cottages by the green and a 12th-century church. Above the shingle beach is stationed the famous lifeboat, saviour of so many lives in danger on the Goodwin Sands.

Wateringbury, *Kent,* (Tour 3), is a once-charming village marred by traffic. Pelicans, the oldest building in the parish, contains stone from the old London Bridge, brought by barge by a former Lord Mayor of London. The gardens of Wateringbury Place include a terraced chain of lakes and a sunken rose garden. In the church vestry is an oaken staff with an iron point at one end and a ring at the other, known as the Dumb Borsholder of Chart, a symbol of authority of the Hundred Courts.

***Weald and Downland Open Air Museum,** *W Sx,* (Tour 12) is at Singleton and has an unusual collection of historic buildings – houses, barns, workshops etc – which have been removed from their original sites and re-erected. The museum covers over 40 acres. Parking is free, and there are picnic sites and pleasant woodland walks.

West Chiltington, *W Sx,* (Tour 11). The early-Norman church has had little addition since medieval times, and one of the murals is thought to be contemporary with the original building. In front of the churchyard is a whipping post, restored for the Festival of Britain, and a small private museum. There has been modern but tasteful development south of the village, where an 18th-century smock mill has been partially restored.

Westerham, *Kent,* (Tour 6) is the most westerly town in the county; although on the A225, the M25 has relieved it of much of the heavy through traffic. The church tower is Early English, with the arms of Edward VI, unique in Kent; also unique is the 14th-century spiral staircase. On the green are statues of Sir Winston Churchill (see Chartwell) and General James Wolfe, Westerham's most famous men, with several attractive old houses behind it.
*Quebec House (NT) was the boyhood home of General James Wolfe, although he was born at Westerham Vicarage. The square brick house is low lying, and was badly damaged by flood in 1968. The rooms are full of Wolfe memorabilia.
*Squerryes Court is a 17th-century redbrick house, home of the Warde family. As a boy General Wolfe, who lived nearby at

Quebec House, was friendly with the Warde children, and an urn in the garden is said to mark where he was first commissioned. The house contains some fine pictures, including a portrait of Wolfe. Behind the house is the park, where the Darent rises.

West Firle, *E Sx,* (Tour 9). This small village lies at the end of a cul-de-sac. The 13th-century church is comparatively large; its most impressive feature is the tomb of Sir John Gage, who built Firle Place, and his wife Philippa.
*Firle Place is a Tudor mansion with 18th-century restorations facing an impressive park, and the home of the Gage family for four and a half centuries. Downstairs is the Great Hall, and an elegant drawing-room supported by gilt Ionic columns. Upstairs the Long Gallery stretches the full extent of the east front. The house contains a fine collection of furniture, porcelain and pictures, the latter largely portraits of the Gage family, including a huge Van Dyck.

South of the village are the Downs and the towering Firle Beacon. The Beacon is over 700 feet high, with a history going back to Neolithic times. Numerous barrows have been excavated on its slopes.

West Hoathly, *W Sx.* High up on the fringe of Ashdown Forest, 6 miles north of Haywards Heath, this little village has magnificent views to the north and south. In the village centre are the 13th-century church, with an unusually heavy oak door, and the Cat Inn, a hostelry much frequented by smugglers in the past. Ashdown Forest was iron country, and the iron tombslabs in the church and the fireplace furnishings in the inn are of local origin. Further along the road is the 15th-century Priest's House, now a small museum run by the Sussex Archaeological Society and including old furniture and an assortment of oddities from the past. North of West Hoathly is Gravetye Manor, an Elizabethan house set in woodland, whose owner at the beginning of the present century was William Robinson. Robinson was a well-known landscape gardener, and did much to improve the house and its grounds. Gravetye is now an hotel and country club, noted for the excellence of its food and wines.

West Malling, *Kent,* (Tour 6) is a small town with a wide main street and buildings in a variety of styles; Tudor, Elizabethan, Georgian. The Abbey was destroyed, along with the old village in 1190 and was rebuilt as a Norman nunnery; today part is occupied by Anglican Benedictine nuns and part by Anglican

91

Cistercians. Just south of the town is St Leonards Tower, a fine 11th-century Norman keep and once part of the manor house of Bishop Gundulph of Rochester. It is open to the public at all times. During the expulsion of Asians from Uganda by Idi Amin in 1972 large numbers were housed in the married quarters of the airfield, famous during the Battle of Britain.

West Tarring, *W Sx,* is one of the villages engulfed by the spread of Worthing, but it has managed to retain something of its village character. A row of 15th-century half-timbered cottages is now a museum run by the Sussex Archaeological Trust. The village school occupies the remains of a palace of the Archbishops of Canterbury, and tradition has it that Becket stayed here. The 13th-century church is massive, with a battlemented tower.

Westwell, *Kent,* is a remote village on the Pilgrims' Way, 4 miles northwest of Ashford. The church is Early English, with a vaulted chancel and a forest of stone columns; Richard Barham, author of the *Ingoldsby Legends*, was curate here early in the 19th century. East of the village is Eastwell Park, one of the biggest and most attractive in Kent, with an 18th-century ornamental lake popular with anglers and an 18th-century gatehouse with little to commend it but its size,

Whitstable, *Kent,* is a seaside holiday resort and boating centre on the north coast. It has an attractive front, with rows of weather-boarded fishermen's cottages, and inland a medieval church that has been much restored. Once Whitstable was a port for Canterbury, connected to it by a railway, and famous for its oysters. Now both the railway and the oysters are gone.

Wickhambreaux, *Kent,* (Tour 1), is one of the loveliest villages in the county. Away from main roads, it is largely unspoilt, with its tiny tree-shaded green, its little houses opening directly on to the streets and its Hooden Horse Inn, a centre for Morris dancing. The church is 15th century. An old weather-boarded windmill stands at a crossing of the Little Stour.

Wilmington, E Sx, (Tour 9). The remains of an 11th-century priory, now merged into a farmhouse, houses an agricultural museum. Above the village, cut into the chalk of the Downs and marked with white concrete blocks, is the famous Long Man, a gigantic figure 240 feet high holding a stave in each hand. His origin is uncertain, but he is believed to date from Celtic times.

Wincheslea, *E Sx,* is a peaceful place, largely residential, on the A259, 8 miles northeast of Hastings. Where neighbouring Rye is all traffic and sightseers, Winchelsea is comparatively free of both. Like Rye it was invaded by the sea in the devastating 13th-century storm, but being more exposed the damage done was greater and the town was abandoned and rebuilt further inland. Over the next two centuries it was repeatedly raided by the French, and it was in one of these raids that much of the church was destroyed. Yet what remains is beautiful, with superb tombs in the north and south aisles; the stained glass windows are modern, designed as a memorial to the men of Rye and Winchelsea and the Cinque Ports who died in the First World War. A tree on the west side of the churchyard marks where John Wesley preached his last open-air sermon, in 1790.

Land Gate, Winchelsea

Wisborough Green, *W Sx,* (Tour 11) is an open village with a fine 13th-century church overlooking the village and the green. During 19th-century restoration several murals were uncovered, as well as an ancient altar stone, possibly pagan. Two of the church doors are enormous, and the thickness of some of the walls suggest that they may have been part of a keep. The oak doors of the tower are a memorial to the Canadians killed in the Dieppe raid during the Second World War, which was planned in the village.

Wittering, *W Sx.* East and West Wittering are villages on the Selsey Peninsula. East Wittering is full of chalets, bungalows and caravans; it has a large, rather attractive car-park and provides easy access to the sea. West Wittering is more sedate, with few caravans. Its church of St Peter and St Paul stands on the site of a former Saxon church; much of it is Norman, but a cross cut into stone, discovered during restorations in 1875, is believed to be part of the monastery church of 740 and is displayed in the side chapel. Between the two Witterings is Cakeham Manor, a 16th-century house once owned by the Bishops of Chichester.

Worthing, *W Sx,* is a large residential town and seaside holiday resort. It lacks the history of Shoreham, the bustle of Brighton and the aloofness of Hove, and is much favoured as a pleasant place in which to retire. A small fishing village until the bathing boom started in Brighton, Worthing has spread along the coast and inland up the A24, engulfing the villages of Goring and Salvington and Broadwater among others. There are several rows of elegant houses in the old part of the town near the pier, a good shopping precinct and several swimming pools. Next to the town hall is an excellent Museum and Art Gallery, with a collection of period costumes and furniture. Broadwater's Norman church is noted for its fine carving; naturalists Richard Jefferies and W H Hudson are buried in the cemetery. North of Worthing is Highdown Hill (see above).

Wrotham, *Kent,* (pronounced 'Rutam') is 9 miles south of Gravesend on the A227, at the foot of Wrotham Hill. Although bypassed by the M20 and M26 it still gets plenty of traffic. St George's church is large and spacious, with some fine windows and a clock that is over 350 years old. Opposite the church is Wrotham Place, a gabled Tudor house. Beyond the Bull Hotel, an old coaching inn, are the remains of the old Archbishop's palace. Most of the palace was demolished in Edward III's reign and conveyed to Maidstone to build a new palace there.

Wye, *Kent,* (Tour 2) is a small country town best known for its agricultural college. The latter, founded by John Kempe, a 15th-century Archbishop of Canterbury, who was born in Wye, was originally a college for priests. Later it became a grammar school, and assumed its present role at the end of the 19th century. Wye Downs are a nature reserve, with a great variety of wild life and plants. The large crown on the hillside, best seen from the road to Brook, was carved out by college students to commemorate Edward VII's coronation.

Yalding, *Kent,* (Tour 3), the birthplace of the poet Edmund Blunden, is something of a showplace, with the war memorial at the top of the hill, its oasthouses and weather-boarded buildings, and a beautiful 15th-century stone bridge over the Beult River. The village has become a Mecca for people who like messing about in boats, and at week-ends the Lees is 94 crowded with cars and picnickers.

12 Outstanding Motor Tours

The following pages contain 12 Tours which are felt best to convey the individual flavour of this part of Britain. However, to include in the tours that follow all that the Southeast has to offer would be impossible. There is no visit to the area bordering the Thames Estuary; it has its attractions, but a constant crossing and recrossing of the A2 and M2, or following a route through the conurbation that stretches from Dartford to Rainham, is not a tempting prospect for the holiday motorist. For similar reasons most of the coastal regions have been avoided; they are major roads linking urban areas. But although there are no visits to such historic places as Rochester in the north or Dover and Hastings in the south, most places outside the tours can easily be reached by a short detour from one or other of the marked routes.

Although varying slightly in mileage, any of these Tours should be managed on a couple of gallons of petrol in the average family car. If you wish to cut short, or in other ways vary your route, the Tour Maps indicate where the Tour crosses or is part of the A road network. A separate map on pages 96 and 97 shows this network for the whole area.

The Highlights of each tour are summarized on pages 98 and 99, and draw your attention to the major scenic or architectural places included in each Tour.

The directions given under each map have been set out so that the names of the places you pass through are given a new line, for easy reference. The mileage given after these place names refers to the total mileage from the previous place name.

If a place appears in **bold** type, you will find information about it in the alphabetical list in the Places of Interest section. Certain places eg. **Knowle House** are described under the heading of the nearest town – **Sevenoaks**, in this instance. In such cases a check with the Index at the end of the book, will give the page reference.

You will see that we have in many cases taken you along unclassified minor roads, indicated 'u/cl'. Although this will involve you or your co-driver in keeping a sharper look-out, it also leads to scenic delights you might otherwise miss.

Finally, for those who do not wish to keep rigorously to the routes shown, and in fact for everyone who feels that it is only sensible as well as more enjoyable to have a good map of the area, the up-to-date RAC Regional Map series will give you all the extra information you require.

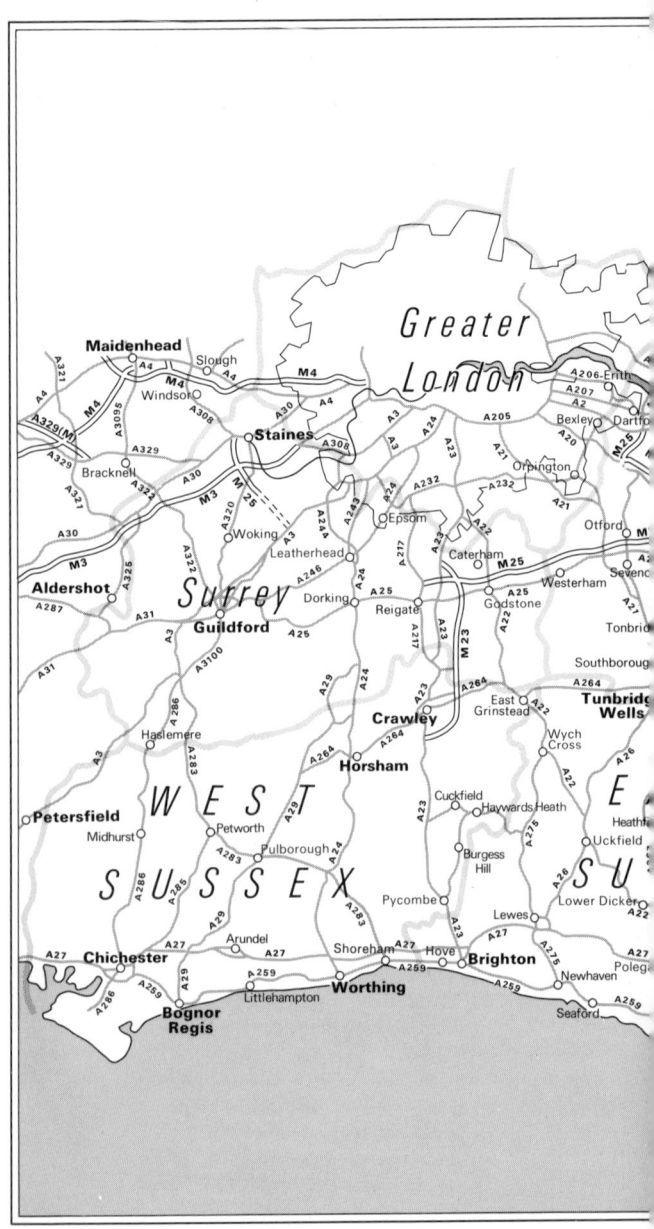

Southeast England

0 miles 10

N

Tilbury
Gravesend
A128
A226
A2
A288
A278
M20
A20
A288
Maidstone
A21
Lamberhurst
A21
Hurst
Green
A265
A21
Sheerness
A288
Sittingbourne
A229
A2
Faversham
M2
Whitstable
A299
Herne Bay
A28
Canterbury
A2
A20
A28
A274
A2
Biddenden
A262
A28
Ashford
A20 M20
A28
New Romney
Rye
A259
Lydd
A259
Bexhill
Hastings

Margate
A28
Broadstairs
A253
Ramsgate
A258
Sandwich
Deal
A256
A20
Dover
Folkestone
A259
Hythe

KENT

T
E X

astbourne

97

Highlights

Tour 1

The tour starts at the fascinating old city of Canterbury. It passes through the ancient port of Sandwich, the Roman fort at Richborough and the lovely villages of Chartham and Wickhambreaux. East of Canterbury the countryside provides wide vistas across the plain with every rise. North and west is largely wooded with places in which to ramble or picnic in Thorden Wood north of Tyler Hill or in East Blean Wood west of Hoath.

Tour 2

This is a scenic tour mainly through downland Kent, with Lyminge Forest and the breathtaking view from the hill above Peene. There is the high woodland drive from Paddlesworth to Acrise followed by the lovely Elham valley. From Bishopsbourne to the Hardres the scenery is delightfully varied the road over Chartham Downs being perhaps the most spectacular in the whole of Kent.

Tour 3

The tour takes in the country around Maidstone, from where many places on the route could form alternative starting points. The northern stretch is through downland country, traversed by winding narrow lanes, largely through woodland, demanding care both in driving and navigation. It includes the Friars in picturesque Aylesford with the Neolithic stones of Kits Coty, the delightful villages of Charing and Yalding, and lovely Leeds Castle.

Tour 4

The tour passes within a few miles of both Ashford and Tunbridge Wells, going through the heart of the Kentish Weald: the '-den' country, where picturesque villages such as Biddenden and Marden mark the early clearings in the old forest. The scenery is varied – hop-gardens and fruit orchards, woodland and farmland – with visits to Sissinghurst garden, the magnificent Bedgebury Pinetum and the 15th-century Godinton Park, a house rich in woodcarving.

Tour 5

Without a visit to Romney Marsh your knowledge of Kent is incomplete. With its remote little villages and its pastureland dotted with innumerable sheep, the Marsh has a fascination all its own. The tour also touches the coast at Camber and Dymchurch, and visits Ellen Terry's home at Small Hythe, with a pleasant walk alongside the stream, and the lovely little town of Rye. The castle and Zoo Park at Lympne are also included.

Tour 6

The northwest corner of Kent is rich in history, and this tour visits among other places the Roman villa at Lullingstone, Knole Park, lovely Ightham Mote, and the garden of Great Comp. From Eynsford to Trottiscliffe the road winds up and down hill, alternating woodland with panoramic scenery. You can walk or picnic in the woods south of Knole or high up in the forest around Toys Hill and at the magnificent viewpoint of Ide Hill.

Tour 7

Here is an abundance of riches: the gorse and heather and woodland of Ashdown Forest, the stark ruins of Bayham Abbey, the homes and gardens of Penshurst and Standen, and the castles of Chiddingstone and Hever. Every mile is a delight, with marvellous viewpoints such as the picnic site between Wych Cross and Coleman's Hatch, or the hill overlooking Weir Wood Reservoir south of East Grinstead.

Tour 8

The tour takes in the eastern part of the Sussex Weald, which is undulating and wooded. It also includes the Pevensey Levels, through which a narrow lane bordered by dykes winds its way across the plain. There are visits to Pevensey Castle, the Roman Anderida, and to the lovely castle at Bodiam; to Battle Abbey, and the Royal Observatory at Herstmonceux. The villages, often typically Wealden, frequently have fascinating, if sometimes legendary, histories.

Tour 9

Starts in the historic city of Lewes. You see the lovely houses of Glynde Place and Firle Place and the picturesque riverside setting of Michelham Priory. You pass the Long Man of Wilmington, and towering Ditchling Beacon, one of the finest viewpoints in the southeast. But perhaps the particular flavour of the tour lies in the little lanes, winding and hilly, through the heart of the Sussex Weald.

Tour 10

This tour of mid Sussex starts almost immediately with the magnificent view across the Weald from Devil's Dyke. It includes Ditchling Common, and the wooded and lakeland country between Ardingly and Handcross. There are the beautiful gardens of Nymans and Leonardslee and the marvellous collection of exotic trees and shrubs in the grounds of Wakehurst Place. Further south are the ruins of Bramber Castle, one among the historic buildings to be visited.

Tour 11

The southern part takes in the South Downs, with a succession of magnificent views; the drive up to the foot of Cissbury Ring should not be missed even by those disinclined to walk to the top. To the north are farmland and woodland, including the forest drive from Fittleworth to Kirdford. There are visits to the great house of Parham, Arundel Castle, and some of the loveliest villages in Sussex, including Burpham and Amberley.

Tour 12

This route is a scenic delight. There can be few more beautiful areas of woodland than those north of Rogate or south of Petworth, and the road from Upwaltham to East Dean is one of the loveliest in Sussex. There are visits to an open-air museum, several great country houses, a Roman palace and villa, the cathedral city of Chichester, and to Bosham, one of the beauty spots of the Sussex coast.

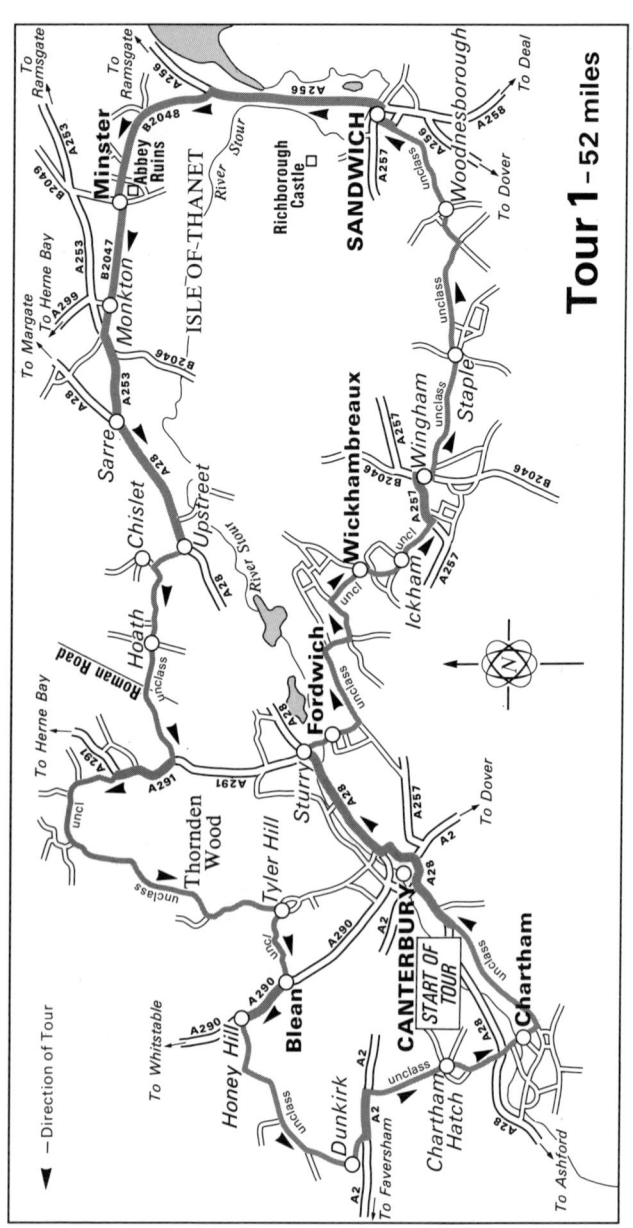

Tour 1 – 52 miles

Tour 1

Canterbury
Leave on A28 (Margate Road).
Sturry 2¼m
Turn R on u/cl road signed
Fordwich ¼m
In ½m turn L at T-junction. In 1¾m turn R. In ½m turn L at crossroads. In ¾m turn R to
Wickhambreaux 3½m
Turn R past church. In 300yd turn L to
Ickham ½m
Leave on road signed Wingham to
Wingham Green 1m
Turn L on A257 to
Wingham ½m
Turn R on B2046. In 200yd turn L u/cl road signed Goodnestone. In 200yd fork L to
Staple 2m
Turn L in village. In 200yd turn R on road signed Woodnesborough. In 1¼m turn L at crossroads to
Woodnesborough 2m

Over crossroads, then turn L to
Sandwich 1¾m
(one way system). Follow sign Canterbury along A257. In ½m turn R u/cl road to
Richborough Castle 1½m
Return to
Sandwich 1½m
Turn L u/cl road signed Ramsgate. In 1¼m roundabout. Take 2nd road, A256. In 1½m turn L on B2048. In 1¼m keep L to
Minster 5½m
Turn L at T-junction on B2047. In 300yd turn R to
Monkton 1½m
In ½m turn L on A253.
Saree 2m
Keep L on A28
Upstreet 2m
Turn R on road signed Chislet. In ¾m turn L at T-junction to
Hoath 2m

Turn L. In ⅓m over crossroads on Hicks Forstal Road. In 1½m turn R on A291. In 1m turn L on road signed Bullock-stone. In 1m turn L on Owls Hatch Road. In ¾m turn L at T-junction
Tyler Hill 8¾m
Turn R then R again to
Blean 1¼m
Turn R on A290. In ¾m
Honey Hill ¾m
Turn L to
Denstroude 1m
In 1¾m fork L. In 1m
Dunkirk 2¾m
Turn L. Then L again on A2. In ½m further turn R u/cl road to
Chartham Hatch 2½m
Turn R at crossroads to
Chartham 1¼m
Over A28. In ¼m turn L at T-junction. In 2m turn L. In ¼m turn R on A28 to
Canterbury 4m

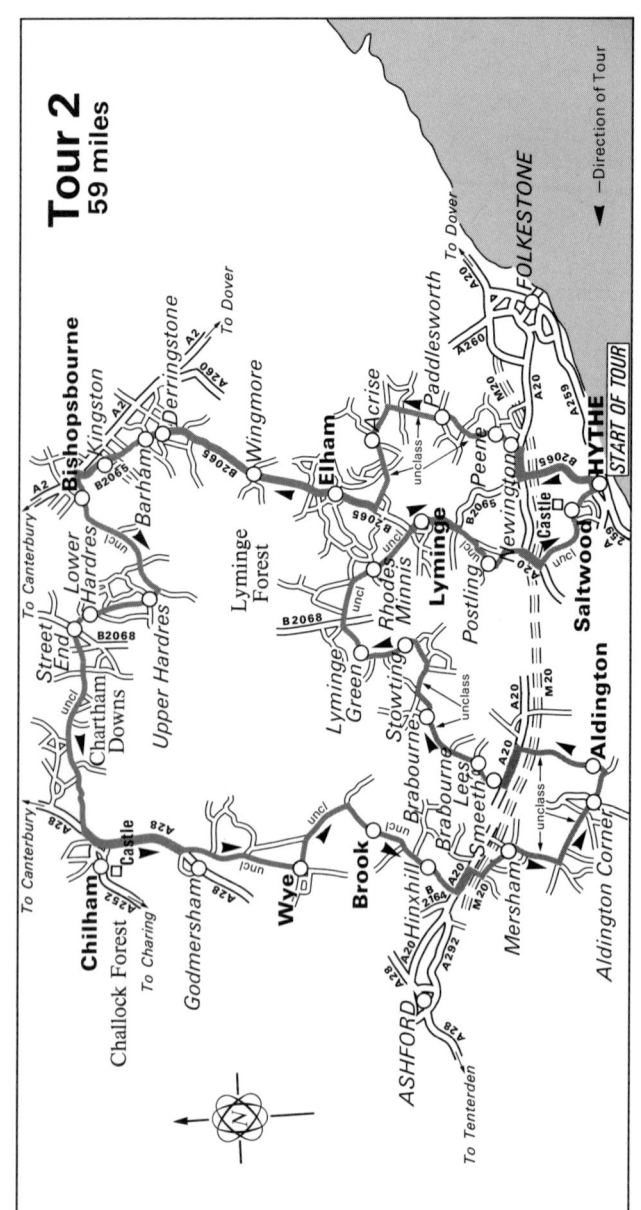

Tour 2
59 miles

—Direction of Tour

FOLKESTONE

START OF TOUR

HYTHE

Saltwood

Aldington

Aldington Corner

Mersham

Smeeth

Brabourne
Lees

Brabourne

Brook

Wye

Chilham
Castle

Godmersham

Challock Forest

To Charing

To Canterbury

ASHFORD

To Tenterden

Hinxhill

Castle
Newington
Postling

Lyminge

Stowting

Lyminge
Green

Rhodes
Minnis

Lyminge
Forest

Elham

Acrise

Paddlesworth

Peene

Wingmore

Barham

Derringstone

Bishopsbourne

Kingston

Lower
Hardres

Upper Hardres

Street
End

Chartham
Downs

To Canterbury

To Dover

To Dover

Tour 2

Hythe
Leave by B2065. Turn R on A20. In ½m L u/cl road signed Newington. Continue to Peene. In ¼m sharp L, then L at T-junction to Paddlesworth. Turn L then R on road signed Acrise. In 1¼m L to Acrise. Fork R signed Elham Valley. In 1¾m turn R on B2065
Elham 9m
Continue through Derringstone, Barham and Kingston. In ¾m join A2, then L u/cl road
Bishopsbourne 6¾m
Turn L signed Bossingham. In 1¼m fork R. In 1½m R to Upper Hardres. Turn R past church to Lower Hardres. Turn L signed
Street End 5m
Turn L on B2068, then R u/cl road. In 2¾m L at crossroads past hospital. In ½m keep R. In ¼m keep L. In 1m L over railway on A28. In ⅓m bear R on

A252, then L
Chilham 5m
Leave by Branch Road. R on A28. In 2m take second turning R u/cl road to Godmersham
Continue past Godmersham Park to cross A28 and railway. In 2½m
Wye 6m
Turn L at crossroads signed Hastingleigh. In ¾m turn R. In im R
Brook 2½m
Hinxhill 1½m
In 1m turn L on A20. In ½m R u/cl road signed Sevington, then L to
Mersham 2m
Turn R at T-junction. In 200yd R again. In 1¼m L at crossroads
Aldington Corner 3¼m
In ¾m turn L
Aldington 1m
Continue to A20, turn L. In 1m R u/cl road to Smeeth and

Brabourne Lees 3m
Bear R at entrance to village. Take second turning L
Brabourne 2m
Turn R in village. In ¼m R at crossroads. In 1m fork L
Stowting 1½m
Turn L to Stowting Common and Lymbridge Green 1¼m
Over B2068 at Sixmile Cottages, follow signs to Elham. In ¼m keep R. In ¾m keep R. In ½m
Rhodes Minnis 2m
In 1¼m turn R on B2065 to
Lyminge 1½m
In two thirds mile over crossroads. In ⅓m fork R
Postling 1¾m
Keep L. In ½m R signed Sandling. Bear R on A20. In ½m L u/cl road
Saltwood 2¾m
Hythe 1m

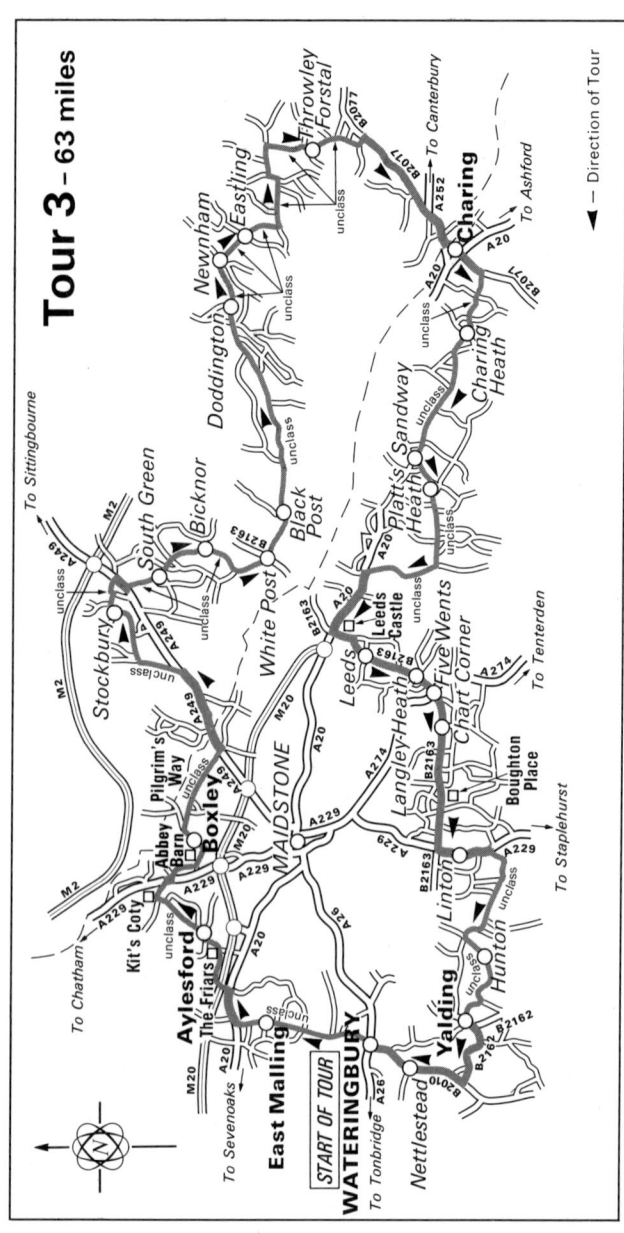

Tour 3 – 63 miles

— Direction of Tour

To Sittingbourne

M2

M2

Stockbury

South Green

Bicknor

A249

unclass

A249

B2163

Black Post

White Post

Newnham

Doddington

Eastling

Throwley Forstal

unclass

unclass

To Canterbury

B2077

B2077

A252

Charing

A20

To Ashford

A20

B2077

Charing Heath

Platt's Heath

Sandway

unclass

unclass

A20

A20

Leeds Castle

B2163

B2163

Five Wents

Chart Corner

A274

To Tenterden

Pilgrim's Way

unclass

A229

Boxley

Abbey Barn

Kit's Coty

The Friars

Aylesford

unclass

M20

MAIDSTONE

A20

M20

A229

A26

A20

M2

To Chatham

A229

Leeds

Langley Heath

A274

B2163

Boughton Place

To Staplehurst

A229

Linton

Hunton

unclass

B2162

Yalding

B2162

B2162

B2010

Nettlestead

East Malling

M20

To Sevenoaks

A20

A26

To Tonbridge

unclass

START OF TOUR

WATERINGBURY

104

Tour 3

Wateringbury
North over A26 u/cl road to
East Malling 2½m
Turn R on A20. In ¾m turn L, signed
Aylesford 2¾m
Over old bridge, detour L to
The Friars ¼m
Return to village, fork L signed
Rochester. In 1½m
Kits Coty 1¾m
R at junction, then R on A229. In ¼m fork L, u/cl road signed Sandling. In ¾m L at crossroads, signed Boxley.
Abbey Gate 1m
Turn R. In 200yd follow sign to
Boxley 2m
R at T-junction, (Pilgrims' Road) signed Detling. In 1¼m, L on A249. In 2m fork L, signed Yelsted. In 1m R, and in 300yd R again
Stockbury 5¾m
Turn R past inn. In ½m fork L. Turn R on A249. In ¼m L, signed Bicknor.
South Green 2m
Keep L through village. In ¼m over

crossroads. In 300yd over crossroads. Keep R past Bicknor church. Over Hollingbourne. Over B2163. In 1¼m over crossroads. In ¾m fork L. In ¼m fork R. In 3¼m
Doddington 7½m
Newnham 1¼m
Turn R signed
Eastling 1m
R at T-junction, then L, signed Throwley. In¾m L. In 1m L again. In ¼m R. In ¾m R again. In 1m fork R. In ¼m R to
Throwley Forstal 4m
In ½m keep L. In ¾m over crossroads. In 1¼m R on B2077. In ½m join A252. In ¾m L on B2077 to
Charing 3¾m
Over A20. In ½m R on u/cl road signed Charing Heath 1¾m
Fork R, signed Lenham. In ½m fork L, signed Lenham Heath. In 2m, over crossroads.
Sandway 2½m
L at crossroads, signed to

Platt's Heath ½m
Fork R, signed Ulcombe. In ½m keep L. In ¾m over crossroads. In ¾m R at crossroads. In 1½m L on A20. In 1½m detour on B2163
Leeds Castle 4m
Continue on B2163
Leeds 2½m
Langley Heath 1m
Five Wents ½m
Over A274 on B2163 signed Boughton. In 2½m on L corner of crossroads
Boughton Place 2¾m
Continue on B2163. In 1m L on A229 to Linton 1½m
In ¾m past church, R on road signed Hunton. In 2m R at T-junction, signed Hunton. In ½m L at T-junction
Hunton 3¼m
Yalding 2m
Turn L. Over bridge, R on B2162. Then R on B2015 to
Nettlestead 3½m
Wateringbury 1m

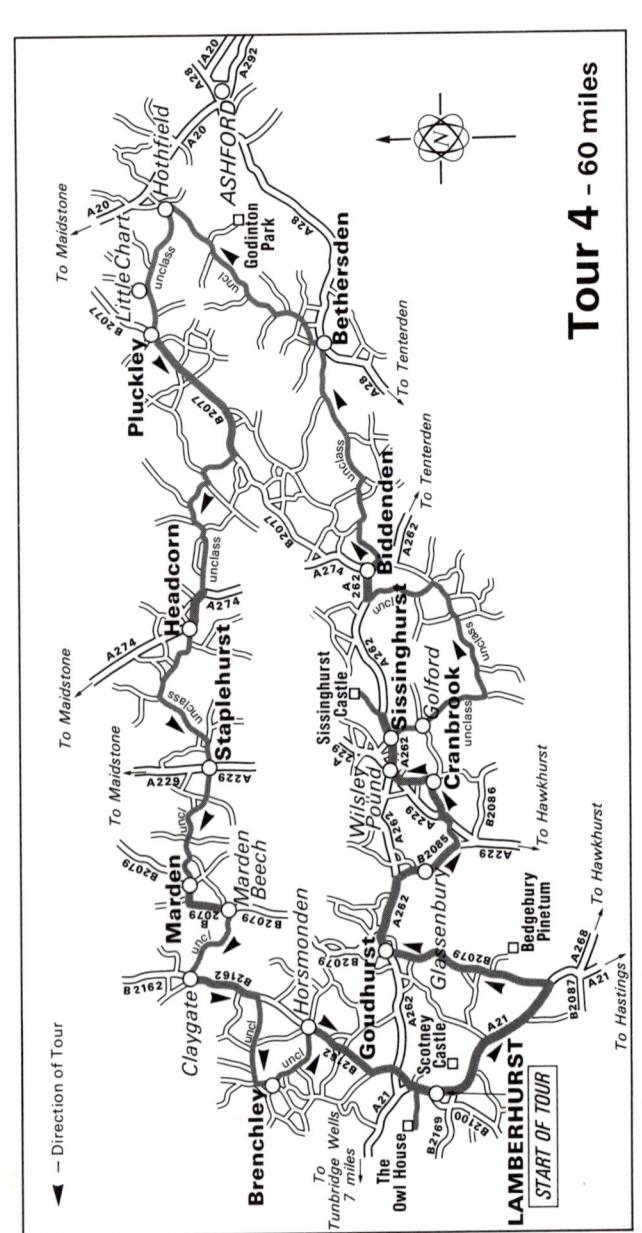

Tour 4 - 60 miles

N

To Maidstone
To Maidstone
To Maidstone

Hothfield
ASHFORD
Little Chart
Pluckley
Bethersden
To Tenterden
To Tenterden
Headcorn
Staplehurst
Biddenden
Sissinghurst
Sissinghurst Castle
Golford
Cranbrook
Marden
Marden Beech
Wilsley Pound
Horsmonden
Claygate
Glassenbury
Goudhurst
Bedgebury Pinetum
To Hawkhurst
To Hawkhurst
Brenchley
Scotney Castle
To Hastings
LAMBERHURST
START OF TOUR
The Owl House
To Tunbridge Wells 7 miles

Godinton Park

▼ – Direction of Tour

A20
A28
A292
A20
B2077
unclass
uncl
A28
B2077
A274
unclass
unclass
A262
A262
A274
A229
A229
B2079
unclass
A229
A262
A229
B2085
B2086
B2079
A262
A21
B2087
A268
A21
A21
B2169
B2100
B2162

Tour 4

Lamberhurst
Leave as for Eastbourne on A21
Scotney Castle ½m
In 3m turn L on B2079. On R
Bedgebury Pinetum 4½m
Goudhurst 2m
Turn R on A262. In 1¼m turn R on B2085
Glassenbury 2¼m
In 1m turn L u/cl road signed Cranbrook. In ½m turn L on A229
Cranbrook 1½m
Wilsley Pound 1¼m
Turn R on A262 at crossroads
Sissinghurst ¾m
Detour L to
Sissinghurst Castle ½m
Return to Sissinghurst, turn L u/cl road signed Benenden. Straight on through Golford crossroads. In 2¼m L on road signed Biddenden. In 2¾m L at crossroads signed Cranbrook. In ½m R and in 1m R again on A262
Biddenden 7½m
R at T-junction end of village. In ¼m turn L u/cl road. In 1¾m R at T-junction signed Bethersden. In ¼m L at T-junction, in 2¼m keep R to
Bethersden 5½m
L on A28, L again on u/cl road signed Pluckley Station. In ½m turn L. In ¼m over crossroads. In ¼m fork R signed Great Chart. In 2m ignore Hothfield turning, turn L in ½m over railway signed Hothfield
Godinton 4½m
Turn L to
Hothfield ¾m
Turn L on road signed
Little Chart 2m
L on road signed Pluckley. In 1m L again on B2077
Pluckley 1m
In ½m fork R, then over crossroads in ½m. Turn L at triangle junction signed Smarden. In 2¾m turn R on road signed
Headcorn 6½m
At village end crossroads turn L u/cl road signed Staplehurst. In 2m L at T-junction to
Staplehurst 4½m
Cross A229 signed Marden. In 1¾m turn R then L to
Marden 2¾m
Keep L on B2079 signed Claygate. In 1m crossroads turn R u/cl road
Claygate 3m
Turn L on B2162. In 1½m turn R u/cl road to
Brenchley 3½m
Keep L. In 200yd past church L to
Horsmonden 2m
Turn R on B2162. In two thirds mile keep R. In 1¾m cross A262. In ½m turn L on A21 then detour R in 200yd
Owl House 3½m
Return to route for
Lamberhurst ½m

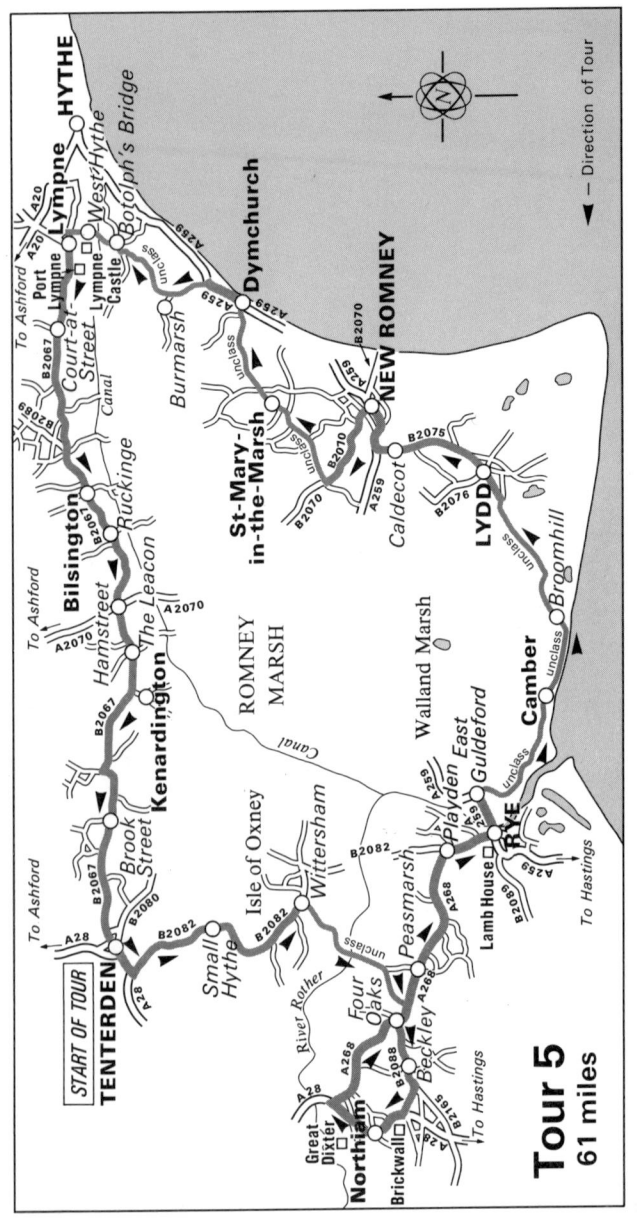

Tour 5
61 miles

Tour 5

Tenterden
Leave as for Rye on B2082 signed
Small Hythe 2¼m
Wittersham 2¾m
Turn R on u/cl road signed Peasmarsh.
In 2½m fork R. In 1m turn R on A268
Four Oaks 4m
Turn L on B2088 signed Beckley
Clayhill 1½m
Keep R. In ¾m turn R on A28
Northiam 1½m
Keep R. In 1m turn R on A268
Four Oaks 3¼m
Peasmarsh 2m
Playden 2¾m
Rye ¾m
Keep L, then turn L on A259. In 1m turn
R u/cl road signed
Camber 4m
Lydd 5m
Keep L on B2075. In 2½m turn R on
A259 signed to
New Romney 4m
Turn L on B2070 signed Ashford. In 2m
turn R u/cl road
St Mary-in-the-Marsh 4m
Leave on road signed
Dymchurch 2½m
Turn L on A259. In 1m turn L on u/cl
road signed Burmarsh. In 1m fork R to
Botolph's Bridge 3½m
Fork L to
West Hythe ¾m
In ½m, turn L on B2067. In 300yd, bear
L to
Lympne Castle ¾m
Return to route. In ¼m
Port Lympne ¼m
Court-at-Street 2m
In 1m keep L. In ¾m keep R. In 300yd
turn L to
Bilsington 3¼m
Ruckinge 1¼m
Hamstreet 1½m
The Leacon 1m
In 1m detour L, u/cl road signed Apple-
dore. In ¼m, turn L to
Kenardington Church 1½m
Return to B2067, turn L
Brook Street 3½m
Tenterden 2½m

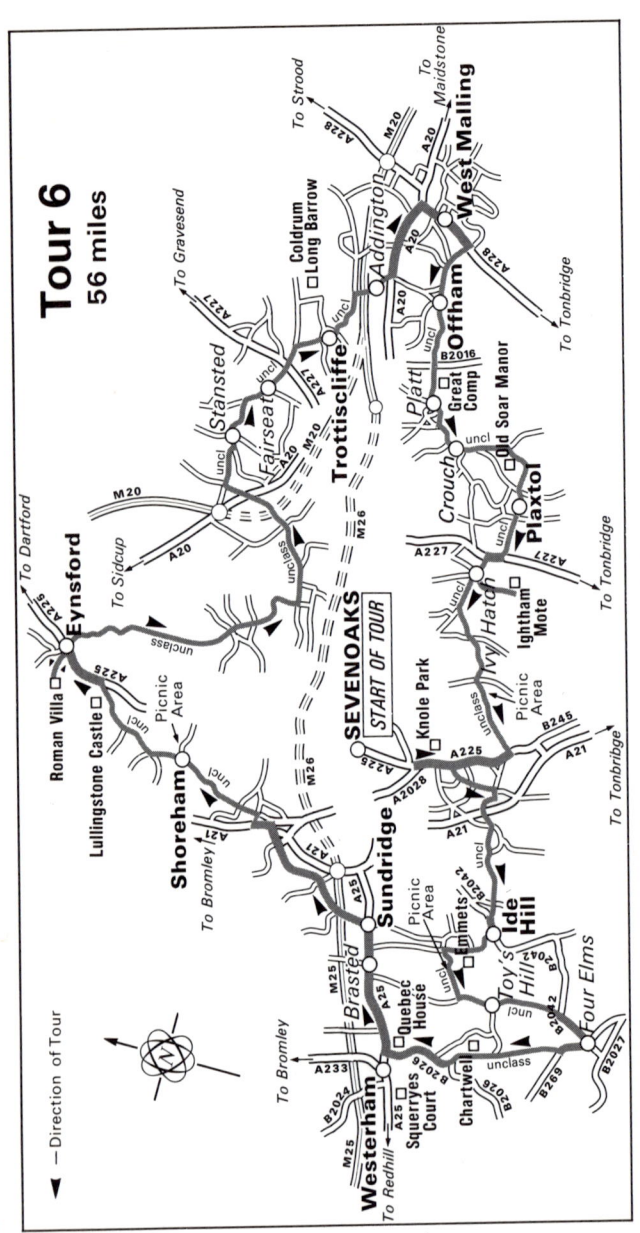

Tour 6
56 miles

To Strood

To Gravesend

To Maidstone

West Malling

M20

A228

A20

A20

To Tonbridge

A228

Addington

Coldrum □ Long Barrow

uncl

A20

A20

A227

Stansted

uncl

Fairseat

A20

uncl

Offham

uncl

To Dartford

M20

Trottiscliffe

M26

Platt □

B2016

A20

Great Comp

Old Soar Manor

uncl

Crouch

Plaxtol

A227

A227

To Tonbridge

To Sidcup

Eynsford

A225

A225

unclass

unclass

Roman Villa □

uncl

uncl

Picnic Area

Lullingstone Castle □

A21

Knole Park

A227

uncl

Ivy Hatch

Ightham □ Mote

Picnic Area

B245

SEVENOAKS
START OF TOUR

A225

A21

To Tonbridge

To Bromley

Shoreham

A225

M26

A2028

A21

Sundridge

A25

M25

Brasted

A25

Picnic Area

uncl

A2028

Emmets

A2028

uncl

Toy's Hill

uncl

Ide Hill

B2042

Four Elms

B2027

To Bromley

A25

Quebec House

B2026

B2026

unclass

B2027

Westerham

M25

Squerryes Court

B2024

A233

Chartwell

B2026

B2042

B269

To Redhill

A233

— = Direction of Tour

N

110

Tour 6

Sevenoaks
Leave on A225 as for Tonbridge. In 200yd L after junction with A2028
Knole ¼m
In 100yd turn R u/cl road Oak Lane. Over crossroads. In ¾m cross over A21 u/cl road to
Ide Hill 3¾m
Turn R in village then on L
Emmetts ½m
In ⅓m turn L. In 1m turn L
Toys Hill 2m
At Four Elms turn R, crossroads B269. In ¼m turn R u/cl road signed
Chartwell 4¼m
Westerham 1¾m
Town mainly on L. Turn R on A25 to
Brasted 1½m
Sunbridge ¾m
L at lights u/cl road signed Chevening, fork R, keep R to join A21 as for London. In ½m R u/cl road signed Otford. In 300yd turn L
Shoreham 4¾m
(Detour down Church St to bridge and river walk.) Turn R at T-junction signed Eynesford. In ¾m R signed Well Hill to
Eynesford ¾m
Detour L over bridge to
Lullingstone Roman Villa
Lullingstone Castle ½m
Return to route. R at War Memorial u/cl road. In 3m over crossroads signed Woodlands. In 200yd turn R. In ¼m over crossroads. In 1m L signed Wrotham. In two thirds mile L signed West Kingsdown. Cross A20 u/cl road signed Ash. In ½m R at crossroads
Stanstead 8½m
Turn R at T-junction to Fairseat. Cross A227. In ½m R
Trottiscliffe 3¼m
Detour L at crossroads
Coldrum Long Barrow 1¼m
Return to crossroads, L then fork L
Addington 2½m
Turn L on A20, R on A228
West Malling 2m
In ½m R on Teston Rd
Offham 1¼m
Fork L in village, over B2016 signed Platt. In ½m
Great Comp 1¾m
In 1m over crossroads to Crouch. Keep L. In 1m R signed
Old Soar Manor 2½m
In ½m turn R
Plaxtol 1½m
Turn R signed Ightham. Turn L at church. In ¾m R on A227. In 300yd L to Ivy Hatch. Detour L to
Ightham Mote 2m
Return to Ivy Hatch. Turn L. Fork L by Plough Inn, L again
Stone Street 1¾m
Fork L signed Bitchet Green. In 2½m R on A225
Sevenoaks 4½m

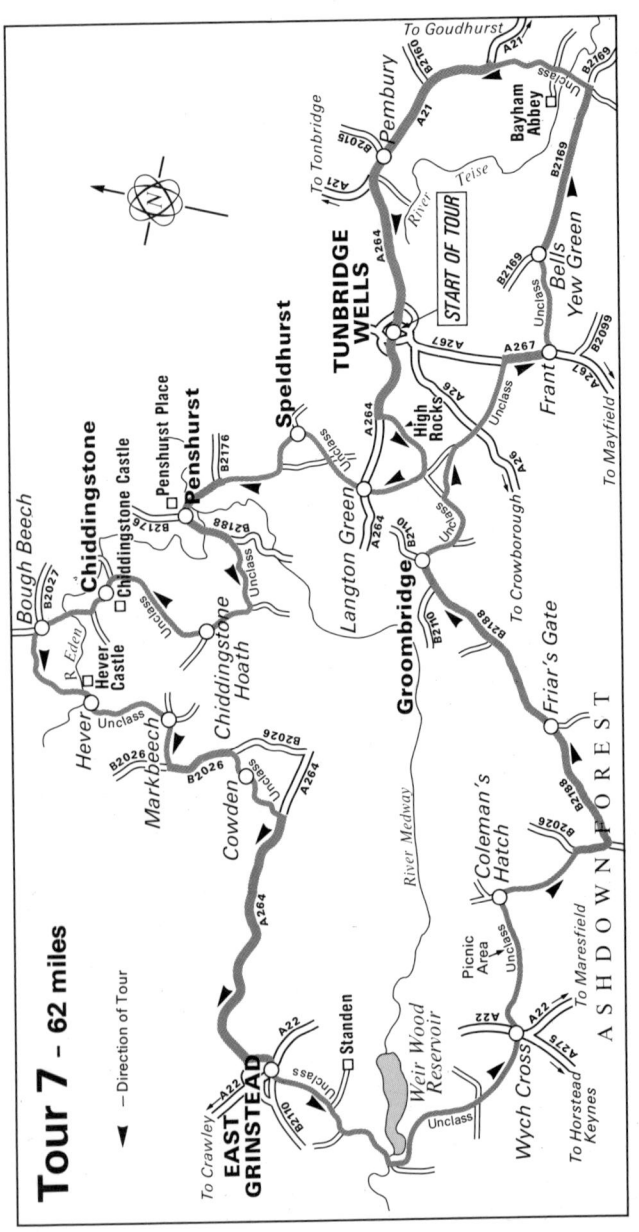

Tour 7 – 62 miles

◄ – Direction of Tour

Tour 7

Tunbridge Wells
Leave by A264 signed East Grinstead. In ¾m past Spa Hotel fork L u/cl road signed
High Rocks 2¼m
In ½m fork R. In ⅓m turn R at crossroads
Langton Green 1¾m
Cross A264, follow u/cl road signed
Speldhurst 1½m
Turn L past church, signed Penshurst
In 1¾m turn L on B2176 to
Penshurst 3¼m
Keep L on B2188, signed Fordcombe. In ½m R signed Chiddingstone Hoath. In 1¼m R at T-junction
Chiddingstone Hoath 3½m
For R, signed Chiddingstone. In 2m fork L
Chiddingstone 2¼m
Detour L at crossroads to
Chiddingstone Castle ¼m
Return to route. Over crossroads
Bough Beech 1½m
Turn L on B2027. In 200yd fork L u/cl road to
Hever Castle 1¾m
Hever ¼m
In ¼m L at crossroads to
Markbeech 1½m
Keep R past church. In ¾m turn L on B2026. In 1m R to
Cowden 2¼m
Continue through village. In ¾m fork R to A264. In 4m L signed Turner's Hill.
Turn R on A22
East Grinstead 5¾m
In 100yd keep L of Island, turn L (Portland Rd). In ⅓m L at T-junction then R at roundabout (Dunnings Rd).
In 1m detour L
Standen 1¾m
Return and fork L u/cl road signed West Hoathly. In 1m L over bridge signed Narrow Road. In 2m over crossroads signed
Wych Cross 4½m
Over A22 at crossroads. In 1m picnic site. In 1½m
Coleman's Hatch 2½m
Sharp R at Hatch Inn signed Newbridge. In 1½m keep R on B2026. In ½m sharp L on B2188
Groombridge 8½m
Sharp R, u/cl road signed Eridge. In ½m bear L signed Tunbridge Wells. In 1m fork R signed Frant. In 1¼m R then L over A26. In 1¼m R on A267
Frant 5m
Turn L on road signed to
Bell's Yew Green 1½m
Turn R over railway on B2169. In 2⅓m detour L u/cl road
Bayham Abbey 3¼m
Return to route. In ½m L at crossroads signed Kipping's Cross. In 1¾m L on A21
Pembury 6m
Turn L at lights on A264
Tunbridge Wells 1¾m

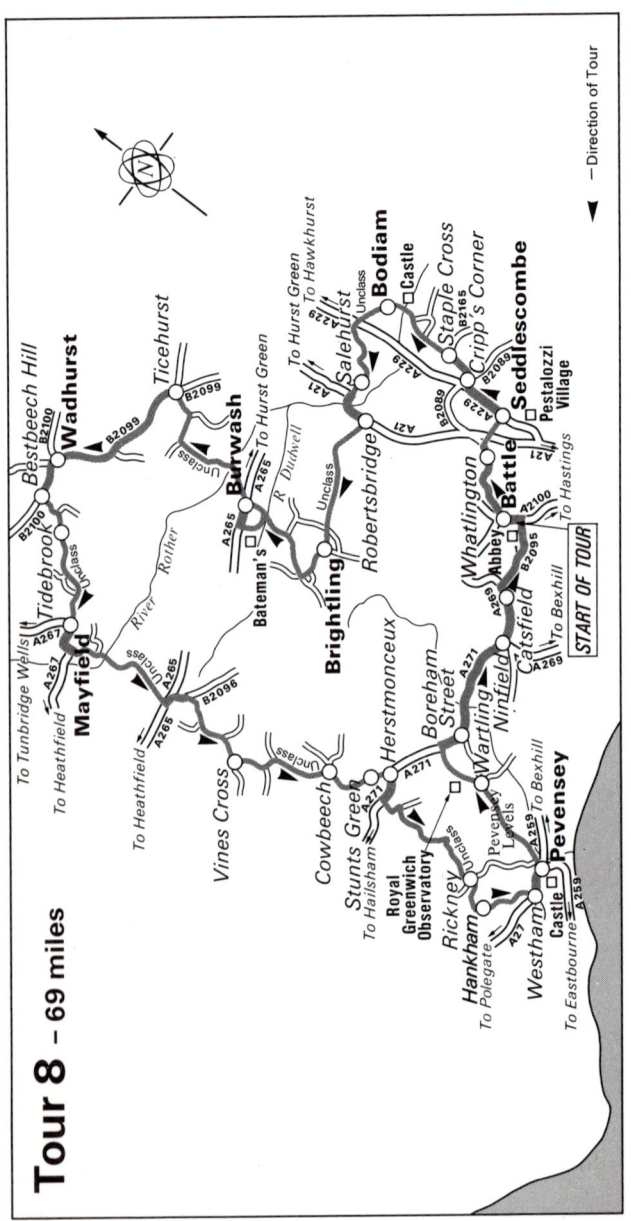

Tour 8 – 69 miles

Tour 8

Battle
Leave as signed Whatlington. Through village, turn R. Over A21 down Stream Lane to
Sedlescombe 3m
Detour R on A229 to
Pestalozzi Village 1m
Retrace route but continue to
Cripps Corner 2m
Turn R B2165 signed Staple Cross. Leave on u/cl road signed
Bodiam Castle 3m
Bodiam $\frac{1}{4}$m
Fork L, signed Hurst Green. In 1m over A229. In $\frac{1}{3}$m, turn L. In 1m fork L
Salehurst 3m
Take road signed Robertsbridge turning L A21 to Robertsbridge. Turn R u/cl road signed
Brightling
In 1m turn L. in $2\frac{3}{4}$m
Brightling 5m
Turn R, signed Wood's Corner. In $\frac{3}{4}$m, bear R. In $\frac{1}{4}$m turn R at crossroads signed Burwash. In $1\frac{1}{4}$m turn L to
Burwash $3\frac{3}{4}$m
Turn L on A265. In $\frac{1}{2}$m L u/cl road
Bateman's 1m
Return to Burwash. Turn R on A265, then L u/cl road past church, signed Ticehurst. In $2\frac{3}{4}$m keep R. In 1m turn L to Ticehurst. Turn L on B2099 to
Wadhurst 9m
Turn L on B2100 to
Best Beech Hill $1\frac{3}{4}$m
Turn L u/cl road signed Tidebrook. In $\frac{1}{2}$m turn R at T-junction to
Tidebrook $1\frac{1}{4}$m
Mayfield $2\frac{1}{2}$m
Through village on A267, then fork L. Turn L on A265, then R on B2096 signed Battle. In $\frac{1}{2}$m fork R u/cl road signed Vine's Cross. In $\frac{1}{4}$m turn R. In $\frac{1}{2}$m fork L signed
Vine's Cross 8m
Turn L on road signed Cowbeech. In 1m fork L. In $\frac{1}{4}$m turn R to
Cowbeech 3m
Turn R at T-junction, signed Hailsham, then turn L at crossroads
Herstmonceux $1\frac{3}{4}$m
Turn R on A271. In $\frac{3}{4}$m turn L down Cricketing Lane. In $\frac{1}{2}$m turn L. In $\frac{1}{4}$m turn R on road signed Pevensey. In 3m
Richney $5\frac{1}{4}$m
Turn L. In 300yd turn R to
Hankham $1\frac{1}{2}$m
Westham $1\frac{1}{2}$m
Pevensey $\frac{3}{4}$m
Turn L at village end. In $\frac{1}{4}$m turn R u/cl road to Wartling. Turn L signed Herstmonceux. In $\frac{3}{4}$m
Royal Greenwich Observatory 4m
In 1m turn R on A271 signed to
Boreham Street 1m
Ninfield 3m
Turn L on A269, signed Battle
Catsfield 1m
In $\frac{1}{4}$m turn R on B2095
Battle $2\frac{1}{2}$m

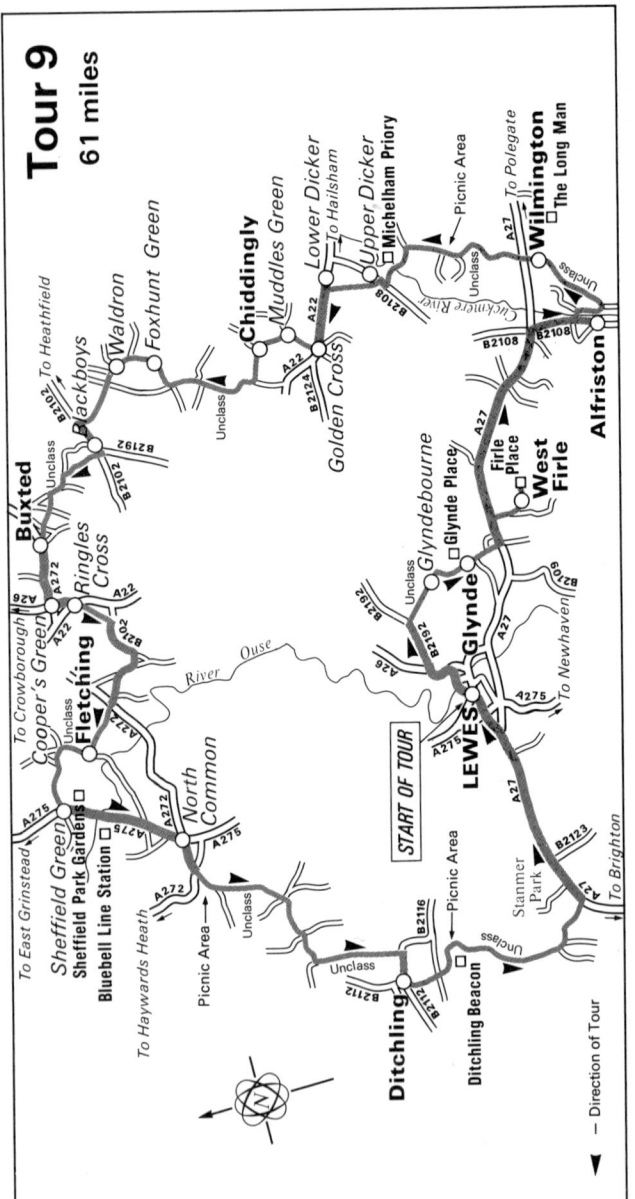

Tour 9
61 miles

To Heathfield

Waldron

Foxhunt Green

Chiddingly

Muddles Green

Lower Dicker

Upper Dicker

To Hailsham

Michelham Priory

Picnic Area

To Polegate

Wilmington
The Long Man

B2108

Cuckmere River

A27

Unclass

Alfriston

B2108

B2108

Blackboys

B2102

To Crowborough

Cooper's Green

A26

Buxted

Unclass

B2102

B2192

Golden Cross

A22

A22

Unclass

B2124

West Firle

Firle Place

Glyndebourne

Glynde Place

Unclass

Glynde

B2192

A27

B2124

B2192

To Newhaven

Ringles Cross

A272

A22

A272

Fletching

Unclass

A272

LEWES

A26

A275

A27

A275

To Brighton

A27

River Ouse

North Common

Sheffield Green

Sheffield Park Gardens

Bluebell Line Station

To East Grinstead

A275

A272

A275

Picnic Area

To Haywards Heath

Picnic Area

Unclass

START OF TOUR

Picnic Area

Stanmer Park

A27

B2123

To Brighton

Ditchling

Ditchling Beacon

B2112

B2116

Unclass

Unclass

B2112

N

▶ – Direction of Tour

116

Tour 9

Lewes
Leave by A26, Uckfield road. Fork R on B2192 signed Ringmer. In 1¼m turn R on road signed Glynde.
Glyndebourne 3¼m
Glynde 1½m
Fork L past station. In ½m turn L on A27. In ¼m detour R signed
West Firle 1½m
Return to A27 and turn R. In 4½m turn R u/cl road
Alfriston 6¼m
Return ¼m. Turn R on road signed Litlington. In 300yd turn R. In ½m turn L signed Wilmington. In 1¼m turn Man on right
Wilmington 3¼m
Cross A27 on road signed Upper Dicker. In 1½m turn R at T-junction. In ¼m forest walk and carpark. In 1m turn L at T-junction
Michelham Priory 3¼m
In ¼m over crossroads signed Golden Cross and in 1¼m
Lower Dicker 1½m

Turn L on A22 to Golden Cross. Turn R u/cl road signed Chiddingly
Muddles Green 2m
Turn L at T-junction to
Chiddingly ¾m
Leave on road signed Whitesmith. Turn R at T-junction signed Waldron. In 2m turn R at crossroads signed Waldron
Foxhunt Green 3¼m
Waldron 1m
Keep L. In ½m turn L on B2102 to Blackbcys 2m
Fork R on B2102 signed Uckfield. Turn R at crossroad u/cl road signed Hadlow Down. In ¾m turn L at fork signed Buxted. In 1m L to
Buxted 3m
Turn L on A272
Coopers Green 1¼m
Turn L at crossroads on A26. In ½m join A22. Turn R down Snatt's Road (u/cl). In ¾m turn R signed Haywards Heath. In 1m keep R. In 1m fork R past pond. Cross A272

Fletching 4¾m
Turn R at church. In ½m turn L at crossroads signed Sheffield Park. In 1¼m turn L on A275
Sheffield Park Gardens 2¼m
In ½m detour R to
Bluebell Line ¾m
Continue on A275. In 2m turn R on A272. In ¾m turn L u/cl road signed Wivelsfield Green. In ½m fork L. In 1½m turn R at T-junction, then L signed Streat. In 1½m turn L on road signed Westmeston. In 2m turn R on B2116
Ditchling 8¾m
Turn L B2112. In 200yd fork L u/cl road signed
Ditchling Beacon 1¾m
In 2¼m turn L at crossroads signed Moulscombe. In 1¼m turn L on A27. In 3¼m roundabout take first road A275 to
Lewes 8¼m

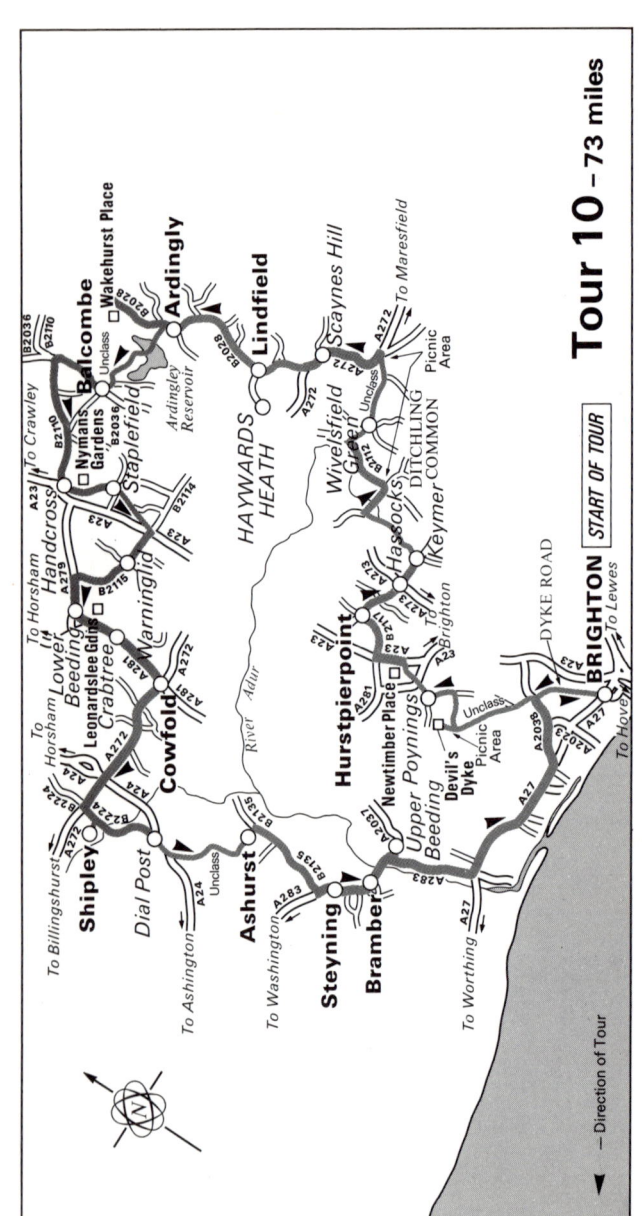

Tour 10 – 73 miles

START OF TOUR

BRIGHTON

To Maresfield

Scaynes Hill

Lindfield

Picnic Area

Ardingly

Wakehurst Place

Balcombe

Nymans Gardens

Staplefield

Ardingley Reservoir

To Crawley

To Horsham

Handcross

Warninglid

HAYWARDS HEATH

Wivelsfield Green

DITCHLING

Hassocks

KEYMER COMMON

Picnic Area

DYKE ROAD

To Lewes

To Brighton

To Hove

Hurstpierpoint

Lower Beeding

To Horsham

Leonardslee Gdns

Crabtree

Cowfold

River Adur

Newtimber Place

Upper Poynings

Beeding

Devil's Dyke

Picnic Area

To Billingshurst

Shipley

Dial Post

Ashurst

To Ashington

To Washington

Steyning

Bramber

To Worthing

— Direction of Tour

N

Tour 10

Brighton
Leave by Dyke Road. Cross A2038 to
Devil's Dyke 6m
Return ½m, turn sharp L signed
Poynings. In 1½m turn L to
Poynings 2¼m
Turn R, signed Pyecombe. In ¾m over
crossroads on A281, signed Brighton. In
¼m turn L u/cl road to
Newtimber Place 1½m
Turn L on A23. In ¾m turn R on B2117
to
Hurstpierpoint 2¼m
Turn R on B2116 to
Hassocks 1½m
Keymer 1m
Turn L at crossroads, u/cl road signed
Burgess Hill. In 2m turn R on B2113,
signed Ditchling. In 1m turn L on B2112
to
Wivelsfield 4½m
Turn R u/cl road to
Wivelsfield Green ¾m

In 2m turn L on A272
Scaynes Hill ¾m
In ¾m turn R on B2111 to
Lindfield 2m
Turn R on B2028 to
Ardingly 3m
Continue on B2028
Wakehurst Place 1½m
Return to Ardingly. Turn R and R again
u/cl road. In 1m fork R at church. In 1m
fork L
Balcombe 4¼m
Turn R. Over crossroads, then R on
B2036 signed London. In 2m turn L on
B2110 to
Handcross 4½m
Keep L on B2114. In 30yd on L
Nymans Gardens ¼m
Staplefield 1m
Bear R at Jolly Tanners. In 1½m turn L
then R onto flyover on B2115 to
Warninglid 2½m
In 2m turn L on A279 to

Lower Beeding
Fork L at Plough Inn. Join A281. On L
Leonardslee Gardens ¾m
Cowfold 2¼m
Turn R on A272. Cross over A24. Turn
L on B2224, signed Shipley. In ½m turn
R u/cl road
Shipley 5m
Return to B2224 and continue to
Dial Post 2¼m
Keep R on A24. After ½m turn L, u/cl
road signed Ashurst. In 2½m fork R to
Ashurst 3¼m
Turn R on B2135. In 2½m bear L on
A283 to
Steyning 3¾m
Bramber ½m
Upper Beeding ¾m
Keep R on A283. Turn L at roundabout
on A27, signed Brighton. In 3¾m turn L
at lights on A2038 (Hangleton Road). In
⅓m keep R. In 1½m R on Dyke Road
Brighton 12m

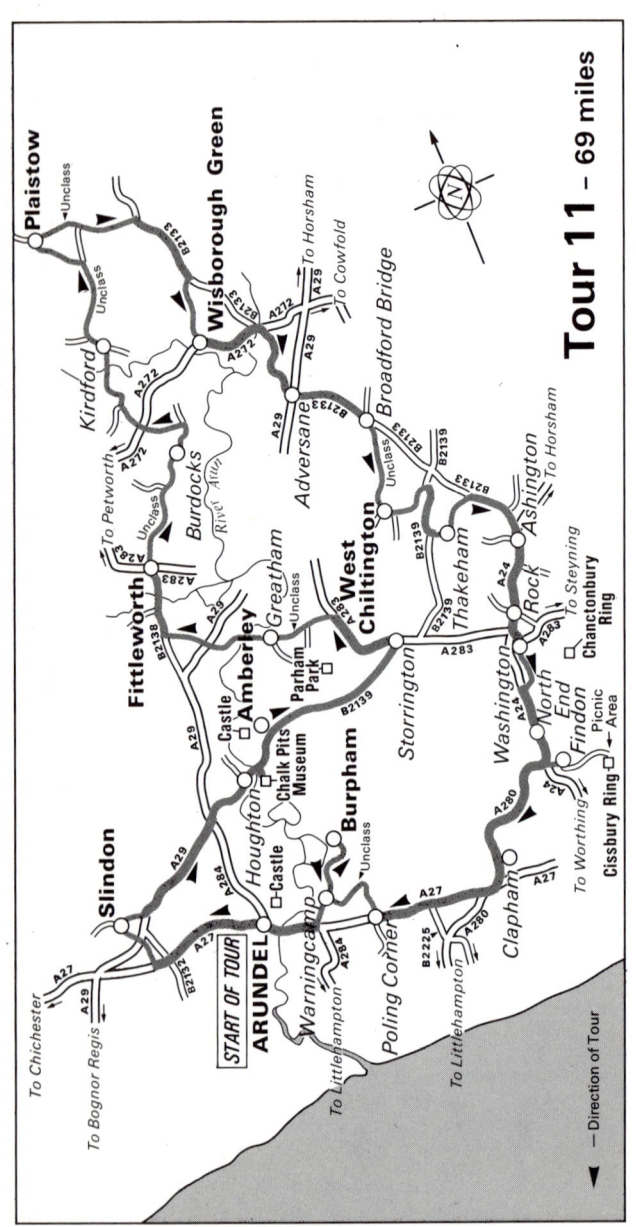

Tour 11 – 69 miles

Plaistow

Wisborough Green

Broadford Bridge

To Horsham

To Cowfold

Kirdford

To Horsham

To Petworth

Burdocks

River Arun

Adversane

Ashington

West Chiltington

Thakeham

Rock

To Steyning

Chanctonbury Ring

Fittleworth

Greatham

Parham Park

Storrington

Washington

North End

Findon

Picnic Area

Slindon

Castle

Amberley

Chalk Pits Museum

Houghton

Castle

Burpham

To Worthing

Cissbury Ring

To Chichester

To Bognor Regis

START OF TOUR

ARUNDEL

Warningcamp

Poling Corner

Clapham

To Littlehampton

To Littlehampton

To Littlehampton

▼ — Direction of Tour

120

Tour 11

Arundel
Leave as for Chichester on A27. Over B2132. In 300yd turn R on Mill Road. Over A29 to
Slindon 4m
Keep R past inn. Turn L on A29 as for Pulborough. At next crossroads take B2139 signed Storrington
Houghton 4¼m
In ¾m Amberley Station
Chalk Pits Museum ¾m
Detour L
Amberley 1m
Return to B2139
Storrington 3½m
Turn L on A283. In ¾m on L
Parham 1m
Continue on A283. In 1m turn L on u/cl road signed Greatham. Continue over A29 as for Fittleworth. Turn R on B2138
Fittleworth 6¼m
Fork L signed Petworth. Turn R on A283 then L on u/cl road signed Bedham. In ¼m fork R signed Wisborough Green. In 1½m fork R signed Wisborough Green. In 1½m turn L signed Kirdford. In ¾m over A272. In ¾m turn R at T-junction signed Plaistow. In 1½m
Kirdford 6½m
Turn L signed Plaistow. In ½m turn R
Plaistow 3¼m
Turn R signed Loxwood. In 2½m turn R on B2133. In 2m turn R u/cl road
Wisborough Green 5½m
Turn L on A272. In 1½m turn R on B2133 signed Ashington. In 1¼m
Adversane 3¼m
Over A29 on B2133. In 2m turn R u/cl road
West Chiltington 4m
Turn L on road signed Thakeham. Turn R, B2139 signed Storrington. In 1½m turn L into village of
Thakeham 2¾m
In 1m turn R on B2133. Keep R on A24 to
Ashington 3m
Continue on A24 as for Worthing. In 2m turn L at roundabout to
Washington 2½m
Return and continue on A24. In 2½m detour L at roundabout to
Findon 2½m
Turn L in village to
Cissbury Ring 1¼m
Return to roundabout. Take 2nd road (A280) signed Angmering. In 3½m turn R on A27. In 4m turn R at Poling Corner on u/cl road signed Blakehurst. In 1½m fork R. In ½m turn R at crossroads to
Burpham 11¾m
To return fork R in village. In ½m turn R at T-junction. In 1¼m turn R. In ¾m turn R again
Arundel 3m

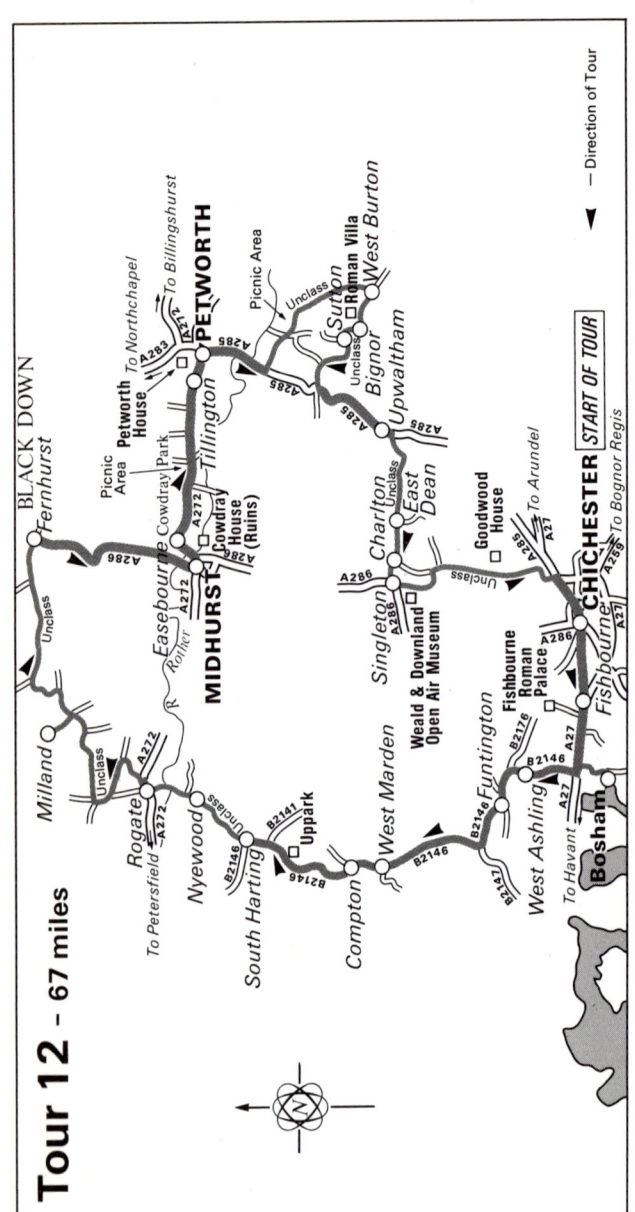

Tour 12 – 67 miles

Chichester
Leave by A259 as for Portsmouth. Join A27

Fishbourne 1¼m
Detour R past Woolpack Inn to Fishbourne Roman Palace ¼m
Return to A27. In 1½m detour L to

Bosham 2½m
Return to route. Over A27, signed Funtington. In 2m turn L to Funtington 5m
Turn R on B2146, signed Harting. In 1m the B2146 turns R to

West Marden 5m
Compton 1m
Keep L on B2146 to

Uppark 2½m
South Harting 1½m
Keep R, then L u/cl road to

Nyewood 2m
Rogate 1½m
Turn R on A272. In ¼m turn L on road signed Terwick Common. In 1m turn L at T-junction. In 1m turn R. In ½m turn R at crossroads. In 2¾m

Milland Marsh 5½m
Over crossroads. In ¼m keep R. In 1¾m turn R to

Fernhurst 4½m
Turn R on A286. In 4½m detour R on A272 to

Midhurst 5m
Return ½m. Leave on A272, signed Petworth. In 2m picnic site in **Cowdray Park** by Benbow Lake. Through Tillington

Petworth 6½m
Turn L at junction with A285 to

Petworth House ¼m
One way through village. Leave on A285 as for Chichester. In 2m turn L u/cl road signed Bignor. In 1¼m over crossroads signed Coates. In ½m fork R to

West Burton 6m
Turn R on road signed Bignor. On R

Bignor Roman Villa 1m
Bignor ¼m
Sutton ¾m
Keep L. In ½m turn R. In 1m keep L. In ½m turn L on A285 to

Upwaltham 4¼m
In ¼m bear R on u/cl road signed East Dean 2½m

Charlton 1m
Singleton ¾m
Keep L on road signed Chichester. Turn L on A286. In 200yd turn L u/cl road

Weald and Downland Open-air Museum
Turn R out of museum and continue on u/cl road. In 1½m Goodwood Racecourse. Over crossroads. In ¾m detour on L to

Goodwood House 2¾m
Return to route. In 1¾m turn R. In ½m turn R on A285

Chichester 3¼m

Opening Times of Important Places of Interest

The dates and times given were correct at the time of going to press. Unless am or pm are specifically shown, places are open throughout the day.

Amberley: Chalk Pits Museum *11am-5pm Wed – Sun*

Arundel Castle *pm Mon – Fri, Apr; pm Sun – Fri, May – Aug*

Battle Abbey *Mon – Sat, also pm Sun; Daily Apr, closed Xmas & New Year's Eve*

Bayham Abbey *See Battle Abbey*

Bentley Wildfowl Gardens *11am-6pm Good Fri – Sep; House: pm also 11am-4pm, Sat Sun, winter*

Bignor Roman Villa *Daily, Mar – Sep. Closed Mon, ex Aug & Bank Hols*

Bodiam Castle *Daily, Apr – Sep; Sun Oct – Mar*

Boughton Place *pm Sat Sun & Bank Hols, early Apr – early Oct; also pm Wed, Aug*

Burwash: Bateman's *pm Daily ex Fri, Mar – May, Oct; also 11am-6pm Mon – Thu, and pm Sat Sun, Jun – Sep; also pm Good Fri*

Charleston Manor Gardens *Daily 11am-6pm, Apr – Oct*

Chartwell *pm Tue Wed Thu, Mar – Nov; also 11am-5.30pm, Jul Aug. Closed Tue after Bank Hol Mon*

Chiddingstone Castle *pm ex Mon; open Bank Hol Mon*

Chilham Castle: *Gardens & Museum only. Daily ex Mon Fri. Jousting display Sun. Banquets Fri Sat Sun*

Cobham Hall *pm Daily Apr; also pm Wed Thu Sun, Aug – early Sep & summer Bank Hol*

   Owletts *pm Wed Thu, Apr – Oct*

Fishbourne Roman Palace *Daily Apr – Nov also Easter & Bank Hol Mon*

Forest Row: Springhill Wildfowl Park *Daily ex Xmas day & Boxing day*

Glynde Place *pm Wed Thu early May – Sep also Easter & Bank Hols*

Godinton Park *pm Sun, Jun – Sep; also Easter & Bank Hols*

Goodwood House *pm Sun Mon, May – mid Oct; also pm Tue, Aug; also pm Easter*

Great Comp Garden *pm Fri Sun Bank Hols May – Oct*

Hever Castle *pm Tue Wed Fri, ex Good Fri, Sun Bank Hol Mon*

Ide Hill: Emmetts: *Gardens only pm Wed Sun, Apr & July – Oct; also pm Tue Wed Thu Sun, May – Jun*

Ightham Mote *pm Fri also pm Sun, Apr – Sep*

Lamberhurst: Scotney Castle *Gardens pm Wed – Sun, Apr – Oct; also Bank Hols, ex Good Fri*

Leeds Castle *pm Tue Wed Thu Sun Bank Hol Mon, Apr – Aug*
Leonardslee Gardens *Wed Thu Sat Sun & spring Bank Hol*
Lewes: Anne of Cleves' House *Mon – Sat Feb – Nov; also pm Sun, Apr – Oct*
Lullingston Castle *pm Wed Sat Sun Public Hols Apr – Sep*
Lympne Castle *Daily, Jul – Sep; also Bank Hol weekends*
Michelham Priory *Daily, May – late Oct; also Easter Hol weekends*
Newtimber Place *pm Thu, May – Aug*
Northiam: Brickwall *pm Wed Sat, late Apr – early Jul*
    Great Dixter *pm Daily, ex Mon Apr – mid Oct; pm last two weekends Oct; also pm Bank Hols*
Nymans Gardens *pm Tue Wed Thu Sat Sun & Bank Hol Mon, Apr – Oct*
Owl House Gardens *pm Mon Wed Fri Sun; also Bank Hol weekends*
Parham *pm Sun Wed Thu Bank Hols Easter Sun – 1st Sun Oct*
Penshurst Place *pm ex Mon & Fri, Jul – early Oct; also Bank Hols*
Petworth House *pm Daily ex Mon & Fri; also Bank Hol Mon*
Pevensey Castle *See Battle Abbey*
Royal Greenwich Observatory (Hertmonceux) *Grounds & Gardens pm Mon – Fri, Good Fri – Sep; Sat Sun Public Hols*
Rye: Lamb House *pm Wed Sat, Apr – Oct*
St John's Jerusalem *pm Wed, Apr – Oct*
Sevenoaks: Knole *11am-5pm Wed – Sat, Apr – Sep & Bank Hol Mon & Good Friday; also pm Wed – Suŋ, Oct – Nov*
Sheffield Park House & Gardens *pm Wed Thu Sun, May Oct;*
Sissinghurst Castle *pm ex Mon & Bank Hols*
Smallhythe Place *pm Tue Fri & Bank Hols, Mar – Oct*
Standen *pm Wed Thu Sat Apr – Oct*
Uppark *pm Wed Thu Sun Bank Hol Mon, Apr – Sep*
Wakehurst Place Gardens *Daily ex Jan 1, May day Hol & Xmas day*
Weald & Downland Open Air Museum *11am-6pm ex Mon Apr – Sep; also, Mon, Jul Aug; also 11am-6pm Wed Sat Sun, Oct; 11am-6pm Sun, Nov Mar*
Westerham: Squerreys Court *pm Wed Sat Sun Bank Hols Mar – Oct*
    Quebec House *pm Sun, Mar; also pm daily ex Thu & Sat, Apr – Oct*
West Firle: Firle Place pm Wed Thu Sun, Jan – *Sep; also Easter & Spring Bank Hols*

Index

This index does not include places with comprehensive information already listed alphabetically in the Places of Interest section, unless as a cross-reference to another part of the book.

RAC Regional Atlas Navigator Series
● 1 South, Southeast, Thames & Chilterns, London ● 2 The West Country, South Wales, Bristol, Cardiff ● 4 Northern England: Lakes, Borders, Leeds, Manchester ● 3 The Midlands (in preparation).
First ever atlases to be compiled from RAC local maps: scale 1.6 miles to 1 inch